DEATH

PARANORMAL
AFTERMATH

HOLLYWOOD
obscura

BRIAN CLUNE

Schiffer Publishing Ltd

4880 Lower Valley Road, Atglen, PA 19310

Book interior designed by Danielle D. Farmer
Type set in Anna/Old English/Machinen/Minion Pro

ISBN: 978-0-7643-5354-3
Printed in China

Published by Schiffer Publishing, Ltd.
4880 Lower Valley Road
Atglen, PA 19310
Phone: (610) 593-1777; Fax: (610) 593-2002
E-mail: Info@schifferbooks.com
Web: www.schifferbooks.com

For our complete selection of fine books on this and related subjects, please visit our website at www.schifferbooks.com. You may also write for a free catalog.

Schiffer Publishing's titles are available at special discounts for bulk purchases for sales promotions or premiums. Special editions, including personalized covers, corporate imprints, and excerpts, can be created in large quantities for special needs. For more information, contact the publisher.

We are always looking for people to write books on new and related subjects. If you have an idea for a book, please contact us at proposals@schifferbooks.com.

Drop of red blood isolated on white background © UserSam2007, Conceptual vector illustration. The bad character traits. Stop addiction © wind art, Murder. Red blood on white background © Yeko Photo Studio, Bloody kitchen knife and blood spots on the white background © Jarek Kilian23, Murder. Red blood on white background © Yeko Photo Studio, Bloody Hand Holding A Bloody Hammer Isolated © shalunx, Handgun Weapon Pistol Firearm Bullet vector icon © briangoff

Other Schiffer Books by the Author:
California's Historic Haunts. ISBN: 978-0-7643-4706-1

Other Schiffer Books on Related Subjects:
In the Company of Evil—Thirty Years of California Crime, 1950-1980. Michael Thomas Barry. ISBN: 978-0-7643-5003-0

Murder and Mayhem: 52 Crimes that Shocked Early California 1849-1949. Michael Thomas Barry. ISBN: 978-0-7643-3968-4

California Ghosts: True Accounts of Hauntings in the Golden State. Preston E. Dennett. ISBN: 978-0-7643-1972-3

Coastal Ghosts of Southern California. Anita Yasuda. ISBN: 978-0-7643-3150-3

THIS BOOK IS DEDICATED TO MY FAMILY WITHOUT WHOSE SUPPORT I WOULD NOT BE ABLE TO CONTINUE WRITING. TO MY WIFE, TERRI, AND MY KIDS, CARMEL, JOSH, AND AMBERLY—I LOVE YOU BANANAS AND GRAPES.

Acknowledgments

I would like to thank my brother and sister-in-law for being my taxi service and driving me all over Hollywood in order to get pictures for this book; it was a lot of fun and there is more to come. I would also like to thank my editor, Dinah Roseberry, for putting up with me and always fielding my thousands of questions with a smile and pleasant attitude—it couldn't have been easy. Last but certainly not least, Bob Davis for always being there, for his generosity and ability to kick me in the butt when needed; I love you my friend!

CONTENTS

FOREWORD

BY BILL MURPHY

Bill Murphy is the st[...] the Syfy Channel's hit s[...] *Fact or Faked: Parano[...]* *Files.* He is also an inde[...] dent film maker, writer, [...] scientist.

HOLLYWOOD. It is steeped in history, sweetened by the dreams its name conjures but tempered by the nightmares that some of the inhabitants endure as they face demons of their own making or become victims of greed. The climate and natural beauty that are fit for a paradise sometimes hide the horror that is revealed when the sun goes down and the makeup comes off. This juxtaposition is analogous to a heaven and hell coexisting in the same place, and in *Hollywood Obscura:*

Death, Murder, and the Paranormal Aftermath, author Brian Clune masterfully sets up the reader by sharing the good (or bad) intentions of the Hollywood hopefuls who are lured by the fleeting promise of fame and fortune only to succumb to the vices that await those who let their guard down. Mr. Clune has exhaustively researched the events that surround the celebrities who are the subject of his book, but has added additional interest by exploring their homes and temporary residences where they took their last breaths. When reading his book, it felt like I was tiptoeing around the rooms and hallways peering into another era, almost like remote viewing through time.

The ability of the author to create an immersive scene was a key to him setting up yet another subtle layer within each chapter. Brian shares in his book that the locations he covers may have become imbued with the essence of the former inhabitants who

lived hard and often died violently, which leads the reader to speculate on the supernatural. I am intrigued by the "stone tape theory," which is the notion that a mental impression can be stored in an environment where a traumatic event has occurred. Even though pundits do not embrace this theory, there is much about the universe that is not known and modern physics cannot fully explain the material world. The reader can decide if the unfortunate demise of the characters in Brian's book have contributed to the strange feelings and odd occurrences reported by visitors to the locations he covers.

Undoubtedly, history buffs and paranormal enthusiasts both will find Brian's book enjoyable, but it is not for the squeamish. Among other things, it contains accounts of bloody confrontations, the discovery of a number of corpses in horrible condition, stories of excessive drug and alcohol use, and every bit of it is real. Perhaps the macabre nature of *Hollywood Obscura* is part of the fascination I experienced while reading his book. There is a morbid curiosity that firmly holds the reader's interest, and I found myself turning each page to learn what fate awaited every individual he writes about. Some people may find every chapter to be a separate cautionary tale, but Mr. Clune does not preach about the lives led by the poor souls in his book, and if anything, he suggests sympathy for the victims. It does make you wish you could have a chance to communicate with those in his book who have lost their lives in such a horrific way. However, Brian's crisp writing style kept me going as he builds momentum quickly, then delivers jaw-dropping details. If you are the type that appreciates a fast paced, riveting book that is biographical, with locations that are historically significant, and includes suggestions of residual hauntings, then this book is for you.

CHAPTER 1
MURDER MOST FOUL

THE DICTIONARY DEFINES MURDER AS:

The killing of another human being under conditions specifically covered in law.

This is a clinical, unemotional definition that can't even brush the surface of the truth of the act. Murder is barbarous, violent, bloody, messy, and destructive, not only for the victims and the killers but to those left behind as well. Throughout history men and women have arisen to kill, some out of passion for a lost love, some over jealousy, most over money and greed. Then there are those, for whatever reason, who have given in to evil, or perhaps they were just born that way; some of these have not only committed murder but have actually enjoyed the act. Others, such as Charles Manson, have used their evil to persuade followers to do their dirty work for them.

California is no stranger to the act of murder; on the contrary, California has produced some of the most vicious and evil mass murderers known to man. The reputation of the state as the land of sun, sand, and starlets has, over the years, been darkened by the knowledge that even the rich and famous are not immune to the whims of the killer. Celebrities and politicians, housewives and gangsters, are all equal in the eyes of the slayer. Lillian Perelson, a housewife from Los Feliz, killed in her sleep with a hammer; Robert F. Kennedy, gunned down just minutes after announcing his run for the White House; Bryan Hartnell and Cecelia Shepard, two college-bound lovers attacked while lying next to a peaceful lake (Shepard was killed, Hartnell was scarred for life); even gangster Bugsy Siegel was brutally gunned down in his girlfriend's Beverly Hills home—all from different walks of life, all with different backgrounds, and all killed easily by people with lesser morals than the rest of society.

There are those individuals in a society who commit murder never realizing or caring that what they are doing is wrong. Their blind hatred for another man's race, their absolute certainty of the guilt of another, even before the facts of the matter are clear, and even the passion of one's belief in their religion have all been causes for the unjust death of another. Vigilantism, in the past has not only resulted in the death of

innocent men and women but is usually overlooked for what it is—organized murder by the masses. A lynching held by an angry mob, a family member out for revenge: These are still just cold-blooded murder, no matter what reasons the perpetrator has to justify the act.

One thing that all murders have in common, from the single act of taking one life to the horrendous brutality of mass homicide, is the disorder and confusion left by the act itself. The living must wrestle with the loss of those taken from them; the how, what, and why of the act; and the regret and uncertainty of what they could have done differently to stop the event from happening. The murderer, in most cases, wants to get away with the act and may, initially, be successful but will inevitably have to live with one eye looking over their shoulder for the rest of their lives in an attempt to either live a normal life or to perpetrate more violence in a sick game of "Catch me if you can." And what of the murder victim? What awaits them after their untimely death?

This may sound like a strange question to the unbeliever; however, for those of us who know that the human spirit goes on, this may be the most important question we can ask. There is a strong belief that when a person has their life violently ripped from this Earth, it can either leave an imprint in the surrounding ether or may actually cause the soul of the victim to remain behind for closure. This closure could be had by helping solve the crime or could manifest in the spirit seeking vengeance from beyond the grave; it is also possible that the act itself has attached the victim's spirit to this realm for reasons we have not yet discovered. Whatever the case may be, I present here just some of the more profound cases in the annals of Hollywood deaths: some proven murders, some thought-to-be murders, and some who may just be cases of fans in disbelief that their idols have left, seeking reasons why they are no longer walking this Earth and entertaining the masses—or so they may think. Each of these cases have one thing in common: The victims have remained behind to continue their story, even after death has found them.

I leave it to you, my intrepid readers, to decide what you believe the truth to be, but in any case, enjoy and keep your minds open to all of the possibilities!

Thelma Todd's Walk of Fame star at 6262 Hollywood Boulevard.

Thelma Todd was one of those rare beauties who also had an abundance of talent to go with her looks. Her comedic flare made her a favorite with moviegoers, and she was much sought after by those in the industry—Laurel and Hardy, the Marx Brothers, and Zasu Pitts to name a few. Dramatic roles were just as easy for her, and the best directors of the time, such as Hal Roach and Roland West, were just as eager to have her in their pictures; she was a star on the rise, but alas, the stars that burn the brightest are those that flicker and go out the soonest it seems.

On a cold December night, Thelma Todd, in a bid to stay warm started her car in a closed garage and turned on the heater. She fell asleep and would never wake up, a victim of a terrible accident — or was it? Even today the tragic death of Thelma is steeped in mystery; was it just an accident or was it murder? There are twists and turns around every corner and a possible curse of her business partner's yacht. The mysterious death of "Hot Toddy" has it all.

Thelma Alice Todd was born in 1906 to John and Alice Todd of Lawrence, Massachusetts. Thelma had one older brother, whom she adored, who was tragically killed in an accident; from that moment on Thelma became the focus of her parent's lives, especially that of her mother. Mourning the death of her brother, Thelma sought out an escape and found it in the form of picture show magazines when she was just twelve years old. It didn't take long for Thelma to fall in love with the movies and stars she was reading about; and then, when she turned thirteen, she saw her first film.

Living on the outskirts of town, it was a short trolley ride to the cinema, and this soon became a weekly outing for Thelma and her mother. They would both look forward to the time spent with each other; this brought them closer together, and later in life would render them nearly inseparable. Thelma began dreaming about one day becoming a big star herself and tried out for all of the school plays and church productions, and was soon appearing on stage in all of them. In high school, she continued to perform but now seemed to have an unending supply of male suitors to choose from; her stunning blonde hair and classic beauty set her apart from most of the other girls at her school. Thelma, however, concentrated on her academics and her acting; she dated but rarely.

After high school, her parents convinced her to continue with her schooling, and she enrolled at the local college pursuing her teaching credentials. To help make ends meet she worked as a substitute teacher and department store model. At her mother's insistence, Thelma signed up for the Lawrence City Beauty Pageant and won. The city then sent her to Boston as their entry in the Miss Massachusetts pageant. Once in Boston, Thelma found herself in strange territory; she found the city to be huge, and at the pageant itself, the media was always underfoot. She soon found herself being interviewed for newspapers and magazines, and they were calling her, "the stunning small-town blonde." All of this attention brought her to the notice of Jesse Lasky, a Paramount Studios executive who had an idea to create a school for aspiring actors and actresses. The best in class would be given a contract with Paramount and a promising career.

At this time in Hollywood things were in turmoil. Fatty Arbuckle had been embroiled in scandal and implicated in the death of Virginia Rappe; director William Desmond Taylor had been brutally murdered; other stars had been found drunk and in *flagrante delicto;* and the studios were in desperate need of cleaning up their image, Paramount being one of those. It was Lasky's idea to experiment with a school that could turn out a young, wholesome group of kids who would be the next big stars in Hollywood, all working for Paramount. After reading about Thelma Todd, he thought she would be a perfect candidate; after meeting her, he was sure of it. Thelma and her mother were taken up to New York during a break in the pageant and given a tour of Paramount's Astoria lot; they were provided with a fine lunch where they were introduced to one of the studio's big stars, Richard Dix, and met some of her future classmates. They then headed back to Boston to finish the beauty pageant, which Thelma won.

While Thelma was in New York going to school, she lived at a hotel for women and was under strict chaperone; her parents rented a small apartment nearby to be close to their beloved daughter. The school was designed to test their acting and star ability, but they were also kept busy with various sports as well. The class was cast in a major film, *Fascinating Youth,* and Thelma was given a minor roll, which she excelled in. When the six months of schooling was over, it was Thelma who was offered the contract at Paramount for one year at a salary of $75 a week, a small fortune for the small-town girl from Lawrence, Massachusetts.

Unfortunately, Thelma's father would not live to see his daughter featured in her first movie; shortly after her graduation, John Todd would have a heart attack and pass away. Thelma and her mother left for New York a few months after his death where she had been cast in her first big picture for Paramount, *The Popular Sin.* After filming was over, they headed west to California and Hollywood where Thelma Todd would try to make her mark on Tinseltown.

Once in the glamour capital, Paramount put Thelma through a grueling year of work. First came the film, *Rubber Heels*; this comedy starring Ed Wynn was not very successful, and once it was a wrap, they immediately cast her in the western *Nevada* opposite newcomer Gary Cooper, *God Gave Me Twenty Cents,* and finally *The Gay Defender*—all of these films in the span of one year. Thelma was now being loaned out to other studios with her salary being raised to $100 a week. She starred in the Universal film *Shield of Honor* and then went to work doing films for 1st National Studios. Her first comedy was the film *Vamping Venus*; unfortunately, the movie had little box office success, and this caused Paramount to drop Thelma's contract. This would be a blessing for her, however, as 1st National was eager to sign her to an exclusive contract.

Although her new studio was eager to have Thelma Todd in their line up, they also wanted certain guarantees from her to justify paying her the $250 a week they were offering. One of the agreements in the new contract stated that she would not exceed 120 pounds or she would be dropped from the studio. Even with this clause, Thelma willingly signed her name. It was right around this time that the silent movie era was coming to a close, and where many other careers were coming to an end because of this, Thelma's was taking off. Her first full sound picture was *Seven Footprints of Satan,* and the film was such a success that her salary was raised to $300 a week. Thelma was also becoming a Hollywood party girl, staying out late at all of the local hot spots and mingling with other stars and directors. She never missed a day's work, however, and this set her apart.

Studio owner Hal Roach, had been following Thelma's career and now thought she would be a perfect fit to appear in Laurel and Hardy's first talkies, and asked for her to be put on loan to him. Her first film with Roach, *Unaccustomed as We Are*, was well received, and Thelma would go on to make at least nine more films with him that year. All in all, Thelma would star in fifteen pictures in 1930, many with Roach as well as 1st National and Pathe Studios. Her success had earned her enough money for her to rent an apartment for herself and her mother in the swanky Knickerbocker Hotel/Apartments. Because of the grueling schedule Thelma had been under, she decided to take a break before moving into the Knickerbocker, and she and her mother went

The Trocadero Night Club where Thelma Todd
spent her last night alive.

back home to Lawrence to spend a few weeks relaxing with family and unwinding from her Hollywood life.

Back in Tinseltown after her vacation, Thelma got right back to work. She had been paired with Zasu Pitts, and together they made a series of successful comedies until Patsy Kelly replaced Pitts. In June 1931, Thelma was again loaned out, this time to United Artists to star opposite Chester Morris in Roland West's film *Corsair*. Roland West wanted Thelma to change her name for the film in an attempt to change her image from a comedienne to that of a dramatic actress. West told everyone on set to address her as Alison. As production continued, Thelma found herself falling in love with West, and that, coupled with her desire to be taken seriously as an actress, she was willing to change her screen name to Alison Loyd. *Corsair* is the only film where Thelma would be billed with this name.

Thelma was now completely in love with the much-older West, and she urged him to divorce his wife, silent screen star Jewel Carmen, so the two of them could be together. West was unwilling to leave his wife but was still quite fond of Thelma. After filming was over, Roland West sailed to Mexico on his private yacht, the *Joyita*, to scout locations for his next film. Roland West always said that the relationship between him and Thelma Todd was not romantic; however, much Thelma might have wanted it that way. He stated that he thought of her as a younger sister; whether this was true or not will now always be speculation. Thelma was devastated, and to ease her pain she would go out every night with her friend, Lina Basquette, ex-wife of Sam Warner. It was on one of these nights that she met the man she would marry and a suspect in her murder just four years later.

Pasquale "Pat" DiCicco was known in Hollywood circles as somewhat of a gigolo; he dated starlets in order to gain recognition and wealth. Thelma, however, either couldn't see the truth or didn't care; West's rejection weighed on her mind, and she may have seen DiCicco as a way to make him jealous enough to change his mind about her. Thelma made sure to be seen with DiCicco and went out of her way to be places with him she knew West frequented. Her ploy didn't work and, with no other options and a true affection for DiCicco, they were married in 1932.

The newlyweds moved into their own apartment, leaving Alice, who adored her new son-in-law, at the Knickerbocker, and at first Thelma was happy and content in married life. Her work at Hal Roach studios was back on track after she made amends to her boss, and Alison Loyd was no more. She starred in movies now with the Marx Brothers and the likes of Clara Bow and even bought herself a brand-new Lincoln Phaeton convertible to be seen in—life was good, at least in the beginning.

Now living at the posh chateau-style Villa Celia apartments, Thelma and Pat began fighting almost every night. It got to the point where the neighbors began complaining and threatening to call the police. Pat had begun to physically harm Thelma, and his abusive demeanor only got worse as time went on. One night, while coming home from the Coconut Grove, Pat drove off the road in a fit of rage, and Thelma suffered a broken shoulder that delayed the start of her new film. While she recovered in the hospital, she made up her mind to leave DiCicco as soon as possible. Once Thelma was recovered enough, production began on *The Devil's Brother*, another Laurel and Hardy comedy; as soon as the film wrapped, Hal Roach sent the stars of the picture to London on a promotional tour, and Thelma was more than happy to be away from her abusive husband. While in England she was offered a role in *You Made Me Love You*, which was to be shot in London, starring Stanley Lupino. This would mean even more time away from home and DiCicco, and so she readily agreed to appear in the film. While in Europe, Thelma was diagnosed with a heart condition; because her father had died of a heart attack, this convinced her even more to end her marriage as soon as she returned home.

As soon as she arrived back in Hollywood, she began making arrangements for divorce. Her first order of business was to create a will, she left only $1 to DiCicco, and this would prevent him from contesting the will. The rest of her belongings she left to her mother. Pat was still unaware of the pending divorce and his antics kept getting both he and his wife spots in the tabloid papers; this was one thing that Thelma couldn't afford to happen to her career, so she pushed headlong into ending her marriage. It would still take until February of 1934 before the divorce was final, and by that time, Thelma had reunited with Roland West.

The "Ice Cream Blonde," as she was now called, was still in high demand, had a huge fan base, and was still very popular with the movie-going public. She starred in fifteen films during 1934, but ever the realist, Thelma knew that as she grew older—if she grew older—the roles would begin to decrease and get smaller, and a younger woman would eventually replace her. To ensure she would have a steady income during retirement she approached Roland West with an offer of a partnership. She proposed that they open an upscale café to cater to the rich and famous; they would use her star power and name to draw in the customers, and his money to fund the venture. West agreed and Thelma Todd's Sidewalk Café was born.

Situated on Pacific Coast Highway, directly across from the beach in Pacific Palisades, the café was an instant success. The restaurant had two levels: a casual yet upscale café on the lower level and a luxury, reservations only, fine dining room on the second floor. While the first floor was almost always filled to capacity with tourists hoping to catch a glimpse of Thelma Todd, the upper room, named Joya's Room, hosted Hollywood's elite along with the rich and famous from all over. Celebrities such as Laurel and Hardy, Walt Disney, Joe E. Brown, and Gloria Swanson were regulars, and Thelma and West couldn't have been happier.

Roland West lived on the hill directly behind the café; it was a bit of a walk up steep stairs but close enough for easy access to the restaurant. Since the café had three levels, Thelma moved into the apartments on the top floor. Roland and Thelma were together every night; West's wife, Jewel, had been in recovery from a nervous breakdown, and West took it upon himself to look after and care for Thelma. They were very private about their lives, and everyone knew that they had separate sleeping quarters, but they also knew that Thelma was never seen dating another man while she was with West. Thelma would still go out almost every night to the clubs unaccompanied, just as she did on the last night anyone saw her alive.

Saturday, December 14, 1935, was the day that Thelma had planned on attending a party for her good friend, Stanley Lupino; she had asked Roland to attend but he had refused. He said that since Christmas was fast approaching, and the crowds at the café were growing, he needed to stay and tend to their guests and urged Thelma to do the same, saying, "They don't come here to see me; they come here to see you." Thelma told him that she was still going to attend her friend's party, and the two had a brief argument before Thelma left to go shopping with her mother. She arrived back at the café around 4 p.m., mingled for a bit downstairs with the guests, and then retired to her apartment to get ready for her evening out. She looked magnificent as her chauffeured limousine picked her up at 8 p.m.: She was wearing a stunning blue evening gown with blue open-toed shoes, diamond rings, hair clips, and a full-length mink coat as she headed off to The Trocadero Night Club.

Thelma thoroughly enjoyed herself at the party; she danced, talked with friends, listened to good music, and drank a lot. The only mar on an otherwise perfect night was when she got into a heated argument with her ex-husband, Pat DiCicco; Ida Lupino, Stanley's sixteen-year-old daughter, had invited him to the party. As the night wore on, Thelma remembered that West had told her to be home by 2 a.m., as he would be closing up the café by that time. She looked at her watch and saw that it was 1:30 and asked Sid Grauman if he would be kind enough to call Roland West to let him know that she was just about to leave the party. She stayed just a bit longer to finish up her conversation and then had her chauffeur take her home.

By the time she arrived home, the café was locked up tight and all the lights had been turned off. Her chauffeur offered to walk her up to her apartment door, but because it was so cold that night, she told him no and to get home and warm up. Thelma made her way up the side stairs, but when she got to the door she found that West had double bolted it, even though he should have known she had left the house with only one key. She knocked on the door for a while, but when West didn't answer, she decided to walk the few blocks to the garage where she knew her Lincoln Phaeton would be parked. She was quite drunk and the climb up the steep stairs in heels couldn't have been easy, but she made it to the garage where she hoped to stay warm until the sun rose in just a couple hours.

Roland West woke up on Sunday morning, but Thelma was nowhere around. Figuring that she had gone to her mother's for the day, he went downstairs, readied the café, and when it was time to open, went about the day's business. Later, when Thelma didn't show up for an arranged dinner party, West began to worry. He asked the staff at the café if anyone had seen or heard from her, but none of them had. By the time he closed that night, there was still no word from Thelma, and West spent a troubled night in and out of sleep waiting for her.

Around 9:30 the next morning, December 16, 1935, Mae Whitehead, Thelma's housekeeper and maid, arrived at the garage to ready Thelma's Lincoln as she did every weekday. This day, however, as she opened the garage door, she noticed that the driver's side door was ajar. She walked up to inspect the car, and that's when she saw the body of Thelma, slumped down behind the wheel with her head resting on the seat. She still wore the clothes that she had worn to The Trocadero two days before, and she was obviously dead.

The coroner's report stated that she had died from carbon monoxide poisoning and ruled it an accident; however, over the years, there has been much speculation as to whether she was murdered, and that there may have been a cover up at the highest echelons of the police force.

One of the first rumors to have spread after Thelma's untimely death was that she had been killed by, or on the orders of, "Lucky" Luciano. The story goes that Luciano and Todd had met one day at the Brown Derby for lunch. During the meal, Luciano explained to Thelma that he wanted to use the top floor of her café as a gambling hall. He explained that it would make both of them rich and place her with some powerful friends. Thelma, not one to shy away from adversity and wanting to make sure she stayed in control of her business, told Luciano to "kiss off" and that he could use her location over her dead body, to which Luciano responded, "That can be arranged."

Some people believe that Luciano was so upset at her rebuff that he instructed his West Coast gambling boss and assassin, Benjamin "Bugsy" Siegel, to kill her. The problem with this theory, however, is that Luciano was nowhere near California at the time he and Thelma were said to have met; as a matter of fact, no record can be found of Luciano ever having set foot in California. They have linked Thelma's ex-husband to Luciano as well.

Pasquale "Pat" DiCicco has been said to be in the employ of the New York mob bosses. Where the rumor was started is now lost in obscurity, but it most likely stemmed from something as simple as his name. Being born in Queens, New York, and having a decidedly Italian name, DiCicco had to be a mobster. Many people believe that he was an "enforcer" for Luciano and is the one who killed his ex-wife on the mob boss's order. There is virtually no evidence that DiCicco was involved with the mob, however. That's not to say he couldn't have killed Todd, just to believe that it had all been a mob conspiracy is a bit hard to swallow.

In 1941, DiCicco married heiress Gloria Vanderbilt; the union didn't last long, and after the divorce Vanderbilt stated that DiCicco was violently abusive. She said, "He would take my head and bang it against the wall." He was a heavy drinker, constantly getting drunk, which would amplify his violent behavior. It is not hard to think that, after Todd divorced him, resentment would set in, and considering the argument at The Trocadero between the two the night Thelma died, it is quite possible that DiCicco finally snapped. He was in New York City when the grand jury, looking into Thelma's death, summoned him to testify. DiCicco said, "Murder or suicide are tenable theories, but I have no idea how Thelma died." The grand jury cleared him of any wrongdoing.

Yet another suspect is Jewel Carmen, Roland West's wife. Everyone knew that she was jealous of the relationship between her husband and Thelma Todd, and having just been released from the hospital after suffering a nervous breakdown, suspicion naturally fell on her. Jewel was staying at the mansion just above the garage where Thelma sought to stay warm, and it would have been easy for her to sneak down and hit Todd in the head knocking her unconscious. That could explain the blood found on Thelma's face and lip during the autopsy. All Carmen would have to do then is leave the garage with the car running and allow Todd to pass away. This is a reasonable theory; however, there is no proof whatsoever that this occurred, and so the investigation was never pursued.

The most widely circulated theory of who murdered Thelma Todd is, of course, Roland West. The story here is that Roland was upset about all of Thelma's affairs and had finally had enough. Another story says that he was trying to gain complete control over the café and felt the only way to accomplish this was to kill Todd. The former story would seem to have no merit, as Todd was never seen with another man in a romantic situation while she was with West; in fact, Thelma seemed to positively worship the man. As far as West wanting full control of the café, one can only speculate. He was already the controlling partner, having put up a majority of the investment money. Also, West knew that Thelma's name recognition was a main draw for the tourists who stopped in to eat, and although the Hollywood crowd were already known to gather at Joya's Room, West knew that Thelma was still one of the reasons they came so often. Whatever the case may be, there are two stories told about how West went about killing Thelma Todd.

The first theory is that upon arriving home later than Roland wanted her to, he flew into a rage and beat her so badly that he feared she was going to die. To try to make it look like an accident, he placed her in the Lincoln, started the motor, and left her there to die. West then called his friends at the Los Angeles Police Department who covered up the incident and had the coroner make no mention of the bruising or other injuries on her body to protect a powerful Hollywood director.

The second story goes that Roland took Thelma out on a late night cruise on his yacht, the MV *Joyita*. This was just a ploy so that West could get her alone and where her murder could not be seen or heard by onlookers. After the deed was done, West snuck her back to the garage where he placed her already-dead body in her Lincoln Phaeton, started the engine, and then left. Again he called his friends at the police who covered up the whole mess, including getting the coroner to lie about carbon monoxide being in her blood.

The entrance to Thelma Todd's Sidewalk Café
as it looks today.

It is reported that on Roland West's deathbed, in 1952, he implicated himself in Thelma's death to Chester Morris; these reports have never been confirmed, and even if he said them, he was in such ill health at the time that he could have said almost anything.

Thelma Todd, in her short time in Hollywood, appeared in 109 movies and shorts; she was a favorite among moviegoers and was loved and respected by those she worked with. Stories about her are numerous, and many of them were written just for the sensationalism and seem far from the actual person and her life. Thelma Todd has become larger than life in death, and the mystery surrounding her passing has over shadowed what was a promising career and her many accomplishments. Maybe that is the reason that Thelma has not passed on but still lingers today in the places she frequented.

PARANORMAL ASSOCIATION

Whether or not Thelma Todd was actually murdered or merely a case of a tragic accident, it would seem that she was not yet ready to pass from this mortal plane. After Roland West divorced Carmen in 1938, he married actress and singer Lola Lane in the 1940s. Roland left the café to her, and when she passed on in 1981, the building became a TV studio for Christian Paulist Productions. Many people, who both worked and acted at the studio, have claimed to see Thelma often. She is usually spotted coming down the stairs; she will sometimes make her way to the outside courtyard where she will stand, seemingly confused, and then will glide towards Pacific Coast Highway and vanish. At other times she will exit the stairs and wander through what was once the lower café. She will stop at times, as if pausing, at a guest's table and then move on to do the same thing, as if she is making her rounds for the tourists.

Upstairs in what used to be Joya's, Thelma has been seen repeating the behavior as in the lower section of the café. The main difference is that when she is spotted upstairs she is usually dressed in an evening gown, and even though her appearance is wispy, one can tell that she is dressed to impress her Hollywood friends. She has also been seen in what were once her apartments on the third floor. Here she is seen not going about the business of entertaining but simply relaxing. Reports from the third floor have Miss Todd simply pacing as if waiting for something, and she has even been seen in casual clothes of the 1930s, including at least once wearing what appeared to be a nightgown and robe. It would seem that Thelma is just as comfortable in her sidewalk café in death as she was while she was alive.

Another place that seems to have paranormal activity relating to Thelma Todd is, of course, the garage where she was found dead. Over the years, visitors going to the spot where Thelma died have reported walking up to the garage and hearing the sound of a car running, even though the door will be open and no car visible. Residents living at the mansion today have had the same experience; reports have come of the sound of a car running in the garage at all hours of the night, but it seems to be more frequent around the hours of 3 to 4 a.m., the same hours that Thelma would have been there trying to stay warm.

Other reports coming from this garage are the smells of carbon monoxide, or in this case, exhaust fumes. People have reported that the gas has become so overwhelming that it has made them sick and has even caused some to have to leave the area for fear of passing out. The fumes appear even though there is no sound of an engine running or even a car in the garage or nearby.

Perhaps the oddest thing to come out of Thelma's death is the possible curse of Roland West's yacht, *Joyita*. Roland West had the sixty-nine-foot yacht specially built in 1931 and named it *Joyita*, Spanish for "little jewel," in honor of his wife, Jewel Carmen. After West began his association with Thelma Todd, the two of them would take numerous trips to Catalina Island, would moor at either Avalon Harbor or The Isthmus, and enjoy the sun and beaches. After Thelma died in 1935, West sold the boat, and it eventually wound up in the US Navy and was used as a patrol boat around the Hawaiian Islands during WWII. In 1943, the boat mysteriously beached itself, but the need for coastal ships made it imperative that the Navy re-float and repair the vessel. The boat was sold in 1948, and cork was added to her hull along with refrigeration equipment, but again the boat mysteriously ran aground. After repair, the *Joyita* was again sold, but the new owner had no use for it and decided to sell it again, this time to a university professor who leased it to her friend Captain Thomas "Dusty" Miller. Miller was a British-born accomplished sailor, but under his watch the *Joyita* would take on a new identity, this one of a ghost ship.

On October 3, 1955, while traveling from Apia in Samoa to the nearby Tokelau Islands 270 miles away, the passengers and crew of the *Joyita* simply vanished. The Royal New Zealand Air Force searched an area of 100,000 square miles, but neither the ship nor any living soul was found. The boat was eventually spotted drifting, partially submerged, on November 10, near the island of Vanua Levu, more than 600 miles from where she should have been. There was no one on board, and the life rafts were missing. On the deck was found a doctor's bag containing a scalpel, stethoscope, and four bloody bandages. The sextant and Captain's logbook were missing along with other navigational aids; someone had erected an awning over the flying bridge, and all of the lights had been left on. Inspection of the radio showed that it had been tuned to the distress band, but it was found that a wire had shorted out. This had drastically reduced the range of the radio, which could account for no signal being received by the Coast Guard or other vessels. Perhaps the strangest thing found onboard, and something no one to this day has been able to figure out, is that the starboard engine was completely covered with mattresses.

Captain Miller was a master sailor and had been on the *Joyita* long enough to know her inside and out. He knew that the cork lining in her hull made her almost unsinkable, and the fact that some of her cargo had been empty, fifty-five-gallon drums made sinking impossible. It is unthinkable that he and his crew wouldn't wait for help on the boat rather than brave the sea in tiny rafts with scared passengers to deal with.

This garage is where Thelma Todd sat in her Lincoln Phaeton to get warm and where her body was found two days after her death.

Many theories have been put forth as to what occurred. They range from mutiny, which could explain the bloody bandages, to pirates, Japanese fisherman angry over losing the war, and even aliens. The facts that no sign of the rafts, missing equipment, people, or missing cargo have ever turned up make all but the alien theory seem plausible. This mystery has caused the MV *Joyita* to become known as the *Mary Celeste* of the Pacific and is even listed in places as one of the top ten ghost ships of the world.

In 1956, the *Joyita* was auctioned off and sold to a Fiji Islander, who overhauled the boat and began fishing charters with her. In 1957, she again ran aground while carrying thirteen passengers; she was again re-floated, repaired, and began sailing a regular trade route between Levuka and Suva Islands. Then, in 1959, she once more ran aground. This time the boat was sold to author Robert Maugham, who wrote the book *The Joyita Mystery* in 1962. Once again, the boat ran aground, but this time would be its last. Sold as a tourist attraction, the *Joyita*, bit by bit disappeared, taken, it would seem, by people wanting a piece of mysterious history; by 1970, the boat was gone with virtually no trace remaining.

While Thelma Todd was alive, the *Joyita* was a yacht that gave pleasure to its owner and friends with no sign of trouble or blight. After her death and the sale of the boat, the *Joyita* brought nothing but pain and death. One wonders if the stories are true that Thelma may have been killed at the hands of Roland West while aboard the yacht and whether her restless spirit was the cause of all of the misfortune following her from owner to owner. Perhaps in Thelma's last gasp of life she cursed the vessel hoping West would be the recipient and thereby granting her some revenge. Whatever the case, looking at what followed the MV *Joyita*, it isn't hard to imagine that the boat truly was a ghost ship.

CHAPTER 3
THE BLACK DAHLIA

The Biltmore Hotel, the last place anyone would see Elizabeth Short alive.

Hollywood. When you think of Tinseltown you think about palm trees, endless sunshine, and, of course, movie stars. The mystique of Hollywood leaves little space for the darker side of human nature; however, Hollywood, with all of its lights, cameras, and glamour has ruined more lives than you can count, and one of the most gruesome, unsolved murder cases in history has a direct link to the "Land of Dreams."

Elizabeth Short was born in Boston on July 29, 1924, the third girl born to Cleo and Phoebe Short. She would eventually have two younger sisters who would look up to her. Elizabeth's father was a successful man who made life comfortable for his family—

that is until the Depression hit. After so many years of a relatively upscale existence, the loss of his wealth hit Cleo hard. He abandoned his family in late 1929 and faked his own death. This left Phoebe as the sole provider, but since times were hard everywhere in America at that time, she was forced to take numerous jobs just to get by. Even while working three jobs, most of their support came from Government Public Assistance programs.

Elizabeth, or Betty, as her family called her, was only five when her father walked out on the family, and the loss hit her hard. She began to escape her life by immersing herself in the films being shown at the movie palaces; by the time she was a teenager, she dreamed about becoming a movie star herself. She was growing up to be a very pretty young woman and had educated herself in the art of sophistication and appearing older than she actually was. She was well liked among her peers, and they were always amazed at how active she was even though she suffered from severe asthma.

Phoebe had received a letter from Cleo a few years after his supposed suicide; he said that he was still alive and living in California. In his letter he apologized profusely for running out on them and begged his ex-wife to let him come home; she flatly refused. Phoebe did tell her girls that their father was alive but also told them that they were not to make contact with him.

When Beth, another one of her mother's nicknames for her, was sixteen her mother worried about the cold Massachusetts winters and sent her to Florida in the hopes that it would help with her asthma. For the next three years, Beth would split time between Miami and Hyde Park. She had been secretly in contact with her father since finding out he was alive, and when she turned nineteen and told him that she wanted to see California, Cleo invited her to come stay with him in Vallejo; she readily agreed. Her mother was not happy when she was told of Beth's plans but wished her daughter well and told her to stay in touch.

Beth Short at that time suffered from bouts of depression, and she was having trouble fulfilling her father's image of what he expected her to be. He began complaining to her about her laziness in keeping the house in order, her inability to find a better paying job, and her dating habits. In an interview after her murder Cleo said, "We set up housekeeping, but she wouldn't stay home. Betty was always running around when she was supposed to be keeping house for me. I made her leave; I told her to go her way, and I'd go mine." So, in 1943, Beth moved out of her father's house and moved to Santa Barbara.

Beth soon found a job at Camp Cook (now Vandenberg Air Force base) in the camp Post Exchange. It didn't take long for the men at Camp Cook to notice their new cashier, and the requests for dates flooded in. Beth, always one to bask in the limelight, grew to like the attention at camp but swore she would never date a serviceman. It was at this time in her life that Beth had her only run-in with the law. On September 23, 1943, while out clubbing with friends, Beth, who normally was not a drinker, decided to join her friends and ordered a cocktail. The crowd that night was a boisterous one, and the barkeep, fearing it would get too out of hand, called the police. Being underage, Beth was arrested, fingerprinted, and booked. This incident figures into the murder investigation later to help identify Short's body.

The arresting officer, Mary Unkefer, took pity on Beth and contacted her mother; Beth was to be sent back to Medford. Unkefer allowed Short to stay with her while transportation was arranged and in a 1947 interview stated that, "She was dressed nicely and was a long way from being a barfly. She had a rose tattoo on her left leg and loved to sit in a way that would allow it to show." Could this be why the killer cut a large chunk of flesh from Beth Short's left leg?

Elizabeth Short sat at the bar in this lobby waiting for her sister as Robert Manley left for home.

Beth returned home but didn't stay long; she went back to Florida and there met a handsome Air Force Lieutenant by the name of Joseph Gordon Fickling. For a girl who swore to never date servicemen, falling in love with him came as quite a surprise. Beth was sure that they would marry, but her plans were cut short when he was shipped over to Europe. They stayed in touch, but it was obvious that he was not going to carry on a long distance relationship with her. Beth was hurt but moved on with her life sure that there was someone out there for her. She may have found that someone.

While still in Florida, Beth met another serviceman and again fell madly in love; he was a decorated pilot who was in Florida training to return to the war to be deployed to the China/Burma/India theater of operations. His name was Matthew Michael Gordon Jr., and he may have been the love of Elizabeth Short's life. The couple hit it off almost immediately, and soon they fell in love. Gordon was shipped out to India, but they wrote to each other almost daily. Major Gordon's airplane crashed on a landing, and while he was recovering from his injuries in the hospital, he sent Beth a letter in which included a proposal for marriage when he returned from the war. Beth, of course, agreed and began making plans for her perfect wedding. Disaster struck on August 10, 1945, when Gordon was again involved in a crash. This time, however, he was killed on impact; it was less than a week before Japan's surrender and the end of WWII.

Beth was devastated. In Matthew Gordon's obituary, it stated that he was planning on returning to Medford to "marry his sweetheart." His parents, however, said that their son never proposed marriage to Short and that she had come asking them for money after his death, and they had flatly refused. Beth, heartbroken and humiliated, returned to California, this time to Hollywood where she would pursue her dream of becoming an actress.

Once Beth had arrived back in California, she moved into the house of Mark Hanson, the owner of the Florentine Club. Beth shared a room with aspiring actress and some say, Hanson's girlfriend, Ann Toth. Toth said of Short, "Betty could not stand up to trouble, and she was always in hot water. She was always well behaved and sweet when I knew her. She was skeptical of people, but even so, she often stumbled into trash." Beth had found out that her former boyfriend, Joseph Fickling, was now stationed in Long Beach and again began a relationship with him. Fickling, however, claimed that it was only a friendship, regardless of what Short may have wanted. Beth would visit him from time to time and stay with him in Long Beach, but Beth could tell that they were not meant for each other. In a letter Fickling received just days before Short's body was found, she had told him she was moving to Chicago in the hopes of becoming a model and to stop sending letters to her at her current address.

In late 1946, Short was in San Diego—what she was doing there is a mystery, but it would seem as if she had no real plans when she arrived, as she was seen many times spending the night at the Aztec Theater, which was open twenty-four hours a day. One of the counter girls at the Aztec, Dorothy French, found Beth Short sleeping in one of the seats, took pity on her, and asked if she needed a place to stay. Beth told Dorothy that she had come to San Diego to look for work because jobs were so hard to find in Los Angeles. Beth agreed to live with Dorothy and her mother for a short "temporary" stay.

While Beth Short was living at the French home she didn't lift a finger to help around the house. She would spend her days on the couch sleeping and then would go out in the evenings to the movies or to nightclubs, where she would frequently pick up men. One of the gentlemen who Beth met was a good-looking redhead from Los Angeles by the name of Robert Manley. They had met one night when Manley had given Beth a ride home from one of the clubs. Beth and Manley went out four consecutive nights before he headed home to his wife and young son back in Los Angeles. With Beth sleeping all day and clubbing all night and refusing to help the household or even look for a job, it all became too much for Dorothy and her mother, and they were forced to kick Beth out right after the holidays.

Once again homeless, Elizabeth Short wired Manley and asked him to come pick her up and take her back to LA. Short told him that she was meeting her sister at the

Biltmore Hotel and asked him to drop her there when back in the city. They stayed overnight in a motel in Pacific Beach where Beth spent the night fully clothed in a chair while Manley slept in the bed. The following morning Manley spent a few hours on the phone making sales calls, and then the two drove back to LA. Once they arrived, Manley helped Short check her bags at the bus station and then drove her to the Biltmore where she was to meet her sister.

When they arrived at the hotel, Beth asked Manley to see if he could locate her sister while she went to the powder room to freshen up. Manley had Virginia (Elizabeth's sister) paged, but she never showed up. It was getting late, and Manley needed to get home to his wife. As it was already dark, he said his goodbyes to Beth Short and headed home. It was 6:30 p.m. on January 9.

It was the last time anyone who knew Elizabeth Short would see her alive.

January 15, 1947, dawned clear and bright in downtown's Leimert Park neighborhood. Betty Bersinger walked down Norton Avenue pushing her young daughter along in her stroller on her way to pick up her husband's shoes. As she strolled along, she thought about how nice the neighborhood would look when they finally finished building the homes in the area now that the war was over. The empty lots along the street had become a dumping ground for people to deposit their trash and old household items they no longer wanted, and it was all becoming an eyesore. Today, she even noticed that someone had dumped a broken storefront mannequin in one of the lots. She spotted it right off because it was so white and looked very lifelike, even though it was obviously broken into two pieces. But as she neared, she realized that what she had taken for a mannequin was the body of a young woman, and she quickly backed away so her daughter wouldn't see what was laying in the tall grass.

What Betty Bersinger found that morning was the mutilated nude body of Elizabeth Short. She had been cut in half at the navel and had chunks of flesh cut out of her abdomen and left leg; one of her breasts had been mutilated as well, and she had been positioned in what investigators assumed was the killers attempt at a seductive pose. Her blue eyes were open, and her legs had been spread in a sexual way with the arms of her torso, which was found a foot away from her lower half, having been raised over her head with the elbows slightly bent. Her face had been cut from the sides of her mouth to her ears in an attempt to give her a permanent smile in death, but perhaps the strangest thing about her naked corpse was that the killer had drained her of blood and had thoroughly washed her body.

The official cause of death from the coroner was blunt force trauma due to a concussion of the brain and loss of blood from the gashes on her face. There were marks on her wrists that indicated that Beth had been tied up, most likely to a chair, and there were indications that she may have been tortured for a few days time.

Having heard the call over the police band channels and being near the scene, reporters arrived on Norton Street before the police. Will Fowler of the *Examiner* even said that he had closed Beth Short's eyes before the police showed up. By the time investigators were on scene, reporters and photographers had trampled over the area and had even touched the body. Each newspaper wanted to be the first to "scoop" the story; competition was fierce among the papers at that time, but on that day, the *Examiner* won out at being the first on the scene. However, it was Beverly Lafayette Means, or Bevo as he was called, a reporter for the *Herald-Express*, that gets the credit for the name the world now knows the case by: The Black Dahlia Murder.

During the autopsy, the coroner found it difficult to get fingerprints from the corpse. This was due to the fingers on Beth's hands being wrinkled from having been in water too long while the killer washed her body. Finally, late in the day, they managed to lift a usable set of prints and planned to send them to the FBI. Due to bad weather, most flights were being cancelled or delayed, and there was no telling how long it might take to get the prints to Quantico. In 1947, it was not unusual for the press to be present during high-profile autopsies, and this case was becoming very high-profile. When the *Examiner* found out that there was a delay, they stepped in and offered to send the fingerprints via their wire photo system; the price for their help was an exclusive on the story. The LAPD agreed, and the following day the FBI matched the coroner's set of prints with the ones the Santa Barbara police had taken when Short had been arrested in 1943.

As the *Examiner* now had the exclusive on the story, they were first, after the police, to learn the identity of the victim, and in one the cruelest tricks a newspaper ever perpetrated against a family, the *Examiner* used their inside knowledge of the case to get information from Phoebe Short, Beth's mother. They called the Short residence in Medford and told Phoebe that her daughter had just won a beauty contest and had called to get information for the news article about the pageant. They asked all types of personal questions going all the way back to Elizabeth's school days. When they were done, they finally broke the news to Phoebe that her daughter had been killed, but Beth's mother refused to believe it until the Medford police showed up at her door. It was Phoebe who would finally identify the body after flying across the country to bury her daughter. Phoebe had trouble identifying the remains, due to Beth's face being swollen and her lips puffy from having been beaten; and the killer had sliced her cheeks open.

By now the Black Dahlia was front-page news and every news service in the nation was scrambling all over California to be the next one to discover something new about the case. Reporters checking out leads in San Diego had found the French family who told them about a man they only knew as "Red." They then combed the area and found the hotel where Manley and Short had stayed before driving back to Los Angeles and now had his address, which they promptly gave to the police. The investigators now had their first concrete lead in the case.

When police approached Robert Manley he looked at them, and before they could even ask him his name he said, "I know why you're here. It wasn't me; I wasn't there." Manley had read about what had happened to Elizabeth Short from the news reports and had figured that it was just a matter of time before the police sought him out. What he hadn't figured on was how the case was about to destroy his life, even though he was innocent of the crime.

Confessions to the crime came pouring in from all over the country; many of them were so wild in scope that it was easy for the police to just eliminate them out-of-hand. But other's, even though the investigators knew they were false, had to be looked into. The waste of manpower and resources was taking its toll. Theories ranged from conspiracies to a lesbian love affair gone wrong. The *Examiner* had recovered Short's suitcase from the bus station and turned it over to the police who found a trove of unsent letters, most addressed to Fickling and Gordon, along with photographs giving an idea of the Dahlia's short life. Then, ten days after the body was discovered, the killer sent an envelope to the *Examiner* that would send chills around the country.

The package that was sent contained the belongings that Short had on her at the time of her abduction; these included her birth certificate, social security card, a membership card to the Hollywood Wolf's Club, a ten-year-old address book belonging to Mark Hanson with some of the pages missing, photos, and the bus station baggage claim check along with the clipping she always carried about her dead fiancé, Major Matt Gordon. The package was addressed using cut out letters from newspaper movie ads and prominent on the front was, "Heaven is HERE," from the ad for the new movie "Stairway to Heaven."

Investigators, using the names found in the address book, began tracking down all of the men listed, seventy-five in all. When asked, they all told variations on the same story; they had met Beth one evening, and she had asked them for money using various excuses for why she needed it, but nothing romantic had ever occurred between any of them. After that one night, they had never seen or heard from her again. On and on the investigation continued, but no concrete leads were ever found, and no suspect has ever been charged with the horrendous crime.

To this day, the Black Dahlia case remains unsolved; there is still widespread speculation, theories, tales, and accusations from all corners of society. John Douglas, one of the best FBI profilers to come out of Quantico, has put together a portrait of the killer and a *Los Angeles Times* reporter, Larry Harnish, has used that profile to come up with perhaps the most compelling suspect to date. He has linked Dr. Walter Alonzo Bayley to every aspect of the profile and has found overlooked associations between Short and the doctor that are hard to ignore. Bayley lived on Norton Street, one block from where the Dahlia's body was discovered. Before he had been kicked out for having an affair, his house on Norton had also been the location where Beth's sister had been married a few years before the killing. He was a prominent surgeon who had the skill and the composure around blood to have performed the bisection and cleansing of Short's body. After Manley had dropped Beth off at the Biltmore Hotel, she had basically been penniless. Being an acquaintance of the family, it is not a stretch to assume Beth would have called Bayley for help as his office was just around the corner from the Biltmore. Beth may have gone over to his place and spurned his advances, which would have sent him into an uncontrollable rage, as the profile suggests, and in that moment may have done something he may not have thought possible: He killed her. Bayley was suffering from early onset of Alzheimer's disease and that, coupled with the stress of his demotion at work and his pending divorce, along with the rejection of a pretty young woman, all fit the narrative of an unwilling, compulsive act. Walter Bayley died a year after the Black Dahlia's murder, which would also account for the killer having never been found.

A witness, the last person to see the Black Dahlia other than her killer, watched as she ascended to this landing before heading to the elevators.

There is much speculation on where the name, "the Black Dahlia" originated; some say her friends gave it to her because she always wore black as a way to be noticed; others claim that the newspapers came up with the name as they were wont to do: names such as the White Orchid Murder, the White Flame Murder, and even the Werewolf Murder. The name actually comes from a soda jerk in Long Beach, California, and his customers. When Short was visiting Joseph Fickling in Long Beach, they would frequent the drug store and its soda fountain; the other customers would always comment on her beautiful dark hair, and the way she would wear it was similar to the actress from the movie *The Blue Dahlia*, which was playing at a nearby theater. Bevo Means learned about the nickname and began calling her the Black Dahlia, and so the papers began using that moniker as well.

PARANORMAL ASSOCIATION

Elizabeth Short's life was one of missed opportunities, bad decisions, betrayal, and death. At the young age of twenty-two, she was killed; the Dahlia had barely begun life when it was brutally and unceremoniously cut short. This may be why the Black Dahlia has not passed on and is to this day still seen at her old haunts.

The area of Leimert Park where the Black Dahlia's body was found is today a place riddled with crime; gang shootings are commonplace, and violence is a way of life. Among all of this there are reports of a woman being seen wandering the neighborhood, naked and in a daze. Her skin is said to be "as white as snow," and her hair is dark and tangled. Could this be the spirit of Elizabeth Short? Paranormal investigators who have braved the area have captured EVPs from the neighborhood of a woman who asks, "Where am I?" and, "How did I get here?" If this were indeed the Black Dahlia, she would seem to be lost and very confused about her death and why she was where she was. Oddly enough, the house that was eventually built on the empty lot where the Dahlia was found seems to have avoided having any spirit activity—at least according to current and past residents.

When Beth Short was working at Camp Cook (Vandenberg AFB today) she lived in Santa Barbara in a bungalow on Montecito Street and Castillo Boulevard. Those living there today claim that the ghost of a very pale woman dressed in black wanders the complex. Could this be the Black Dahlia's spirit? Although she had been gone from Santa Barbara for three years before her murder, she may have returned to the bungalows because it was a place she thought of as home or had pleasant times she wanted to revisit. No one knows for sure why Beth may have come home here or if it is in fact the Dahlia—hopefully some day we will find out.

Another place that the Black Dahlia may have been spotted is in downtown Los Angeles near skid row. I am speaking about the old Greyhound Bus station. Today, the building is a hodgepodge of different tiny shops, but it would seem that the shopkeepers and many of their customers have discovered that there is a spirit wandering about. As with most sightings of the Dahlia, all of the reports from this location tell of a seemingly lost young woman who appears dressed all in black, has very pale white skin and is strikingly beautiful. She has been seen all over the building but has appeared most frequently near the area where the lockers once stood. Could this actually be the spirit of Elizabeth Short looking for her lost luggage? Or could she still be trying to catch her bus to Chicago in the hopes of starting her modeling career in the afterlife?

The place that the Black Dahlia has been seen most often is also one of the oddest places that one would think to look, as she spent virtually no time at the location; however, more reports of her spirit have come from this place than with any of the others. Maybe it is because it was the last place that anyone but the killer can remember seeing Beth alive, or maybe it is the opulence of the location that keeps her here. Whatever the case may be, the Biltmore Hotel seems to be the Dahlia's favorite place in death.

The most famous of these sightings comes from a man by the name of James Moore. Moore was a guest at the Biltmore and was heading upstairs to his room. He waited patiently for the elevator to come down to the lobby, and when the doors opened and he stepped in, he noticed a very pretty young woman had remained in the elevator. His eyes were drawn to her due to her being dressed all in black and having very pale skin. She didn't speak and remained still in the lift but did glance over a couple of times in his direction. When he had pressed the button for the floor he was heading to, he noticed that the panel had already been lit up for the elevator to stop on the sixth floor, so when the doors opened and the woman didn't move he casually spoke to tell her that they had reached her floor. She again glanced at him and then exited the elevator. Just as the doors were closing, she turned back to him and with a look he described as a plea for help started to get back into the elevator. The doors shut before she could re-enter and Moore frantically pushed the button to open the door back up. As the doors slowly opened Moore exited the elevator to see if the young woman needed help, but she was nowhere to be seen. He searched the corridors near the elevator but could find no sign of her. It had taken but a moment for the doors to reopen, and in that time the woman had simply vanished.

James Moore didn't give the episode more than a passing thought, figuring that if the woman had indeed needed help, she would have remained close to the elevator— that is until a couple of days later as he was browsing through a local bookstore. Moore had picked up a book on true crime and mysteries, and while thumbing through the pages, his eye caught a photograph of a beautiful young woman he recognized: It was the same woman he had seen get off the elevator on the sixth floor of the Biltmore Hotel two days before. The only problem was that this woman in the book had died more than fifty years earlier. There was no mistaking the face he was looking at in the book. It was the same woman. At that moment, James Moore realized that the pretty young girl he had ridden an elevator with was none other than the Black Dahlia herself.

The elevators at the Biltmore where guests report
seeing the Black Dahlia's spirit.

James Moore's story is not unique. There have been reports for many years about the phantom young woman who rides the elevator at the Biltmore Hotel. Mr. Moore's just happens to be the one with the greatest detail and panache. One of the myths having to do with the Black Dahlia is that the bartender at the Biltmore was the last person to see Beth Short alive. As Beth was penniless when she had been dropped off at the hotel and was not the floozy the papers made her out to be after her death, it is highly unlikely that this is true; that does not mean that Beth didn't stay for a time at the hotel before her abduction. As mentioned, it is now a widely held belief that Dr. Walter Bayley may have been the killer of Beth Short. Bayley's office was less than a block away from the Biltmore Hotel and the speculation is that Beth had walked to his office after calling him for help. What if Bayley had instead rented a room at the Biltmore for the purpose of giving Beth a place to stay until she left for Chicago? His divorce was not yet final; he still had the money, and he would most likely have used an assumed name. What if Beth had gone to the sixth floor, met Bayley, and when she rejected his advances, he had taken her to a place to be killed. It would explain why the Black Dahlia's spirit has remained at the Biltmore all of these years with no seeming connection.

The Black Dahlia: Mention that moniker and almost everyone knows whom you are talking about. Elizabeth Short: That name might elicit a response ranging from "Who?" to "Wasn't that the Black Dahlia?" It is a sad testimony to our culture that a victim of one of the most horrific crimes of the twentieth century has been relegated to mythical status. Who Elizabeth Short was has been lost over time to misreporting, misrepresentation, and out and out lies—so much so that the truth behind this tragic life has been all but lost. During research for this chapter, I have seen it written that she was a whore, a manipulative temptress, a woman obsessed with fame whose mother never loved her: all of this is just a way to make her and the crime larger than life. The truth is that Elizabeth Short led a life as most of us would: trying to find herself, trying to live her dreams, and trying to survive an uncertain time.

CHAPTER 4

BENJAMIN "BUGSY" SIEGEL

IN LOVING MEMORY FROM THE FAMILY

✡ BENJAMIN SIEGEL FEB 28, 1906 JUNE 20, 1947

Benjamin Siegel's grave marker in the mausoleum at Hollywood Forever Cemetery.

It is said that the only sure things in life are death and taxes, but when your job in life is one of death, killing, and the mastery of avoiding taxes, sometimes divine retribution, or fate if you will, can step in to balance the cosmos. This may be what occurred with Benjamin "Bugsy" Siegel. Even after death his spirit has not found rest. He is destined, it seems, to relive his violent death over and over at the house where he was murdered; he also splits that time at the place that was most important to him, a place he himself built, which also helped create an empire in the Nevada desert.

Born in Brooklyn, New York, to Jewish immigrants, Benjamin Siegelbaum grew up poor in a crime-riddled environment, and learned at an early age that if he wanted to get out of his impoverished life, he was going to have to grow up fast. He was just a teenager when he began threatening pushcart vendors with fellow crook Moe Sedway, extorting money from them for "protection" on New York's Lower East Side, and it is here where he met and befriended Meyer Lansky. Together they formed the Bugs-Meyer Gang, which was to be the start of one of the most famous stories in mob history.

Siegel and Lansky started out as an auto theft team. Siegel would steal the cars, Lansky would get them in good working order, and then they would sell them. They soon branched out to handling hits for bootleggers, and it is here that Siegel found that not only was he good at killing but also actually enjoyed it. This new business would later become the infamous Murder Incorporated, which was responsible for hundreds of contract killings in the 1930s, many of which were performed by Bugsy himself.

As the 1920s drew to a close, Lansky and Siegel decided it was time to expand; to this end they approached Charles "Lucky" Luciano. Luciano was a rising star in the Italian Mafia, and along with notable Mafioso's Frank Costello, Tommy Lucchese, Vito Genovese, Joe Adonis, and Albert Anastasia, they were poised to take over the city's crime empire—and Bugsy and Meyer wanted in on the action. As the 1930s dawned, Joe "The Boss" Masseria had taken over and had placed Luciano as the face of the Family. Luciano was not at all pleased to have the notoriety and the inherent dangers that came along with that notoriety without having the power as well. Luciano decided that if he were going to have the name, he would assume the mantle of Supreme Leader of the American Underworld, and he set in motion his plans to do just that.

On April 15, 1931, Luciano and Masseria were having lunch at the Nuova Villa Tammaro Restaurant in Coney Island. After eating, they relaxed with a few drinks and played cards until Luciano excused himself and headed for the bathroom. As soon as Luciano was out of sight and safe, four men entered the restaurant, pulled out weapons and opened fire on Masseria. His body was riddled with bullets; he died slumped over the table in a growing pool of blood. Luciano then walked out and together the five men left with Luciano in complete charge of the gangs of New York. The four gunmen who walked into Nuova Villa Tammaro that day were Vito Genovese, Joe Adonis, Albert Anastasia, and Bugsy Siegel. Bugsy later bragged that he had fired more shots than the other three men combined and was actually smiling as he left the scene of the crime.

One of the first things that Luciano did upon gaining the throne was to form a National Crime Commission. This was an idea that Siegel and Lansky had brought to Luciano's attention a few years earlier and one that he was now in a position to implement. Once together, this group of the heads of the nation's crime families would control all organized crime in America for years to come. It also made Luciano one of the most powerful men in the world with even Mussolini giving him a wide berth and the respect of a man he knew controlled the crime families of Italy and Sicily as well.

Knowing that Bugsy was a man who could get things done, as well as someone who could be trusted to enforce the will of the Commission, they sent Siegel to

California to take over their West Coast rackets. Once Bugsy arrived, he pushed Jack Dragna, who was at that time in command of the West Coast mob, down to the number two spot and promptly got involved with the Hollywood Extras Union. Siegel would go to the studios and threaten strikes of the movie extras, which would have shut down production and cost the studios thousands of dollars, until they gave in to his demands; and then he would charge the union members a percentage of their raise as a fee for service. All of the money would then go back to New York and the Commissions coffers.

Extortion wasn't the only game Bugsy was playing while in Hollywood, however. Bugsy Siegel was a handsome man and knew it; he was also very charming and knew how to use that ability to get what he wanted. While at the studios, Bugsy would make sure that he would "bump" into the stars wandering around the grounds and would always manage to charm his way into the lives of those he thought important. Celebrities such as George Raft, Clark Gable, Cary Grant, and Gary Cooper were not immune to his charisma, and soon, Siegel was attending dinner parties, movie openings, and private gatherings with Hollywood's elite.

Bugsy was quite the ladies man, and many a starlet found herself frolicking in the mobster's bed: Marie McDonald, Wendy Barry, and even Jean Harlow were known to enjoy his company. Virginia Hill was another in the long line of dames Bugsy bedded, but whereas the others were just diversions or conquests, Virginia seemed to have gotten into Siegel's heart. There is some speculation as to whether she was secretly a mob informant sent to keep an eye on their playboy rackets boss, but Miss Hill would remain his girl until the day he himself was murdered.

In 1939, Siegel received orders from New York crime boss Louis "Lepke" Buchalter that Harry "Big Greenie" Greenberg was hiding out in Hollywood and that he was to be "taken off my list of people to worry about." Siegel knew this meant he was to be killed, and Bugsy went about planning the hit like a child planning a birthday party.

On November 22, 1939, Thanksgiving eve, Greenberg was gunned down outside his apartment building as he arrived home from running a nightly errand. Five bullets were fired, all five found their mark in Greenberg's head, and he died instantly. This was the first mob killing to have taken place in California, and to this day, there are reports of people hearing gunshots on the sidewalk where Greenberg was murdered, and residents of the apartment complex have reported seeing the spirit of a man wandering the property as if lost. Could this be "Big Greenie"?

Bugsy was eventually arrested for the murder along with Whitey Krakower, Siegel's brother-in-law, Allie Tannenbaum, and Frankie Carbo. When the indictments were handed down, Siegel's lawyer found out that Krakower and Tannenbaun had "turned canary" as a way to avoid prosecution. Just before the trial was to begin, Krakower was found murdered; this was meant as a message to Tannenbaum, who had fled to another state, that if he testified in court, he would be killed as well. The case against Siegel fell apart after Tannenbaum refused to testify, and he was released, a free man once again.

Bugsy tried to restart his life after the incident with Greenberg, but found that, even though he had not been convicted, his reputation had been damaged beyond repair with his Hollywood pals, and none of them would give him the time of day. The crime bosses back in New York thought it best to get Bugsy out of California for a while and sent him to Las Vegas to help oversee their gambling ventures in the desert.

The Flamingo Hotel and Casino as it looks today.

Las Vegas at that time was already a gambling town but was still very small and underdeveloped. Siegel had passed through Vegas a few times and had been trying to convince the Crime Syndicate that the oasis in the Nevada desert could become much more than just a way station for people on their way to California. Bugsy envisioned a grand gambling town that the Mob would control and he would oversee. After Siegel arrived in Las Vegas, the Syndicate told him to scout out possible locations suitable for building a resort that would cater to the rich and famous and net the syndicate millions in gambling money. He found the perfect place, and best of all, it was already being developed.

Publisher and entrepreneur Billy Wilkerson had already begun building a first-rate hotel and casino on what would become the Las Vegas Strip—the only problem was that he was running out of money. Wilkerson it seems had a gambling problem, and to help pay off the building loans, he tried to win money at the craps tables. Unfortunately, luck was not on his side, and he lost almost all of his money, including his loan payments. Bugsy Siegel had frequented Wilkerson's Hollywood night club, Ciro's, and the two had become friends, so when Wilkerson told Siegel about his money trouble, Bugsy was quick to jump on the opportunity. He talked his New York Mob friends into making an offer on the casino that Wilkerson couldn't refuse. The Mob offered $1 million, which was accepted, and they then had controlling interest in the resort, and Bugsy would oversee the construction and run the casino when it was completed.

Bugsy had his own ideas on how the place should look and demanded the best of everything. The Flamingo, as it would be called, would be the first resort tourists would see driving out from Los Angeles and, therefore, it needed to shine. There is a myth that Siegel named the resort after his girlfriend Virginia Hill, but the name had already been established before Bugsy and the Mob became involved. Siegel wanted a Parisian-themed showroom, nightclub, and restaurants with the best chefs money could buy, a steam room, athletic room, and air-conditioning throughout the entire resort. He also decided that there was going to be a championship golf course and shopping that catered to the rich and famous right on the resort grounds.

This obsession with luxury was not cheap; his $1.5 million budget grew to a final cost of $6 million. Needless to say, his childhood friend and Mob accountant, Meyer Lansky, and the rest of the Syndicate back in New York were not happy. To try to please his buddies back east, Bugsy pushed up the grand opening of the resort by six months. The Flamingo officially opened its doors on December 26, 1946. In the showroom were such notables playing as Rose Marie, Jimmy Durante, and Xavier Cugat and his orchestra. In the crowd were George Raft, Sonny Tufts, George Jessel, and George Sanders. All in all, the opening of the grand resort was a complete flop.

On opening day, only 105 rooms out of 250 were ready; they were still painting the hotel lobby, plastic curtains covered much of the area, and tarps littered the floors. There was a bad thunder and lightning storm blanketing the region, and those A-listers not grounded from their flights decided not to brave the long drive in the inclement weather. Those who did make it to the Flamingo were up on their luck, and the casino lost an estimated $300,000 the first two weeks the casino was open. Soon after the opening, Bugsy closed the resort and decided to finish the construction and hire a new manager and publicist, Hank Greenspun.

The Flamingo reopened in March 1947, and this time the opening was a success. Many of the Hollywood elite came out to see "Ben's" new resort, and with the hotel rooms finished as well as the whole of the resort, they liked what they saw. By this time, Bugsy was living at the Flamingo in a suite just as opulent as the one reserved for the cream of the elite guests, and was finally living his dream life; this was to be short lived, however.

Even though the Flamingo was at last turning a profit, it wasn't happening as fast as his Mob investors thought it should. There was some speculation among the Bosses that Siegel was skimming some of the profits with the help of Virginia Hill. Even though they had no proof of the embezzlement, for the Mob, the thought of disloyalty was usually enough to convict. The Syndicate called a meeting in Havana, Cuba, to discuss the situation. It was decided that Siegel had out lived his usefulness, and with his childhood friend, Meyer Lansky, casting the deciding vote, a death order was put out for Bugsy Siegel.

Virginia Hill called Siegel and asked if he could come out to her Beverly Hills home and housesit for her while she was away in Europe. Bugsy, always paranoid, was wary of leaving his apartment with its bulletproof glass, escape tunnels, and twenty-four-hour on-call driver but agreed to it nonetheless. On June 20, 1947, while reading the *Los Angeles Times* on the couch in Hill's living room, a volley of gun shots rang out. Bugsy was hit nine times: one round entered his nose from the right and exited his left cheek. The pressure of the bullet going through his skull caused his left eye to be blown out; it was found fifteen feet away from his body. Al Smiley, one of Siegel's close friends, was sitting across from the couch and watched the entire event take place but was completely unharmed by the bullets whizzing around the room.

Benjamin "Bugsy" Siegel, the man who had been part of the Hollywood crowd, playboy ladies man, and one of America's most notorious and meanest Mob figures was dead at the age of forty-one. At the same time as the gunshots were leaving the M1 Carbine rifle in Beverly Hills, Moe Sedway, Gus Greenbaum, and Morris Rosen walked into the Flamingo casino and seized control of the resort. There may be a twist to this story, however; the Mob may not be the ones who killed Bugsy.

Virginia Hill's Hollywood home where Bugsy Siegel was brutally gunned down and where even today his ghost is said to run from unseen assailants.

Even though at the meeting in Havana it had been decided to have Siegel "put on ice," it may have been an act of passion and self-preservation that beat the Mob to the punch. Moe Sedway was responsible for keeping track of the money used to build the Flamingo. Sedway, ever loyal to Lansky, kept him apprised of all of the mishandling of the funds. When Siegel found out that one of his best friends was seemingly betraying him, Bugsy erupted into one of his famous fits of rage and stated, "I want Moe gone! I'll have Moe shot, chop his body up and feed it to the Flamingo Hotel's kitchen garbage disposal." Sedway, though he was best friends with Bugsy, had always lived in fear of Siegel's temper; now, with the threat looming, Moe became terrified, and so did his wife, Bee. Here is where it gets a bit convoluted. It seems that Bee, Moe's wife, had met a man by the name of Mathew "Moose" Pandza and wanted to marry him due to the fact that Moe already had a mistress who he was in love with. Moe wanted to meet Pandza, and after they met, the two became as close as brothers and had decided to share Moe's wife, which was fine with Bee. In an interview from the October 2014 *Los Angeles Magazine*, the son of Moe and Bee Sedway, Robbie, admitted the truth behind the murder of Bugsy Siegel.

Scared that Siegel would follow through on his threat to kill her husband, Bee went to her lover and asked him for help. Moose went to Moe who told him, "Moose, he's got to be gotten rid of. What other answer is there?" Pandza knew that Moe was telling the truth and so began practicing with his military surplus M1 Carbine rifle in the sand dunes of El Monte until he felt he was ready to accomplish the deed. So, on the night Siegel was killed, Moose crept over the flower garden, rested the rifle on the windowsill, and put nine slugs into the infamous Bugsy Siegel. Or so it is alleged.

No matter who it was that viciously gunned down Bugsy Siegel, Moose Pandza or a Mob hit man, there is one thing that we know from the man's violent life and death: Benjamin Siegel is not now, nor may he ever be at rest.

PARANORMAL ASSOCIATION

The Flamingo Hotel was Siegel's crowning accomplishment; it may have also been his eventual downfall. One thing is certain, without Bugsy, Las Vegas, Nevada, may not be the same city we see today. This could be one of the reasons why Bugsy has decided to remain in the resort after his death.

The hotel he built is gone, replaced by a much newer, much glitzier tower; where the old building stood is now a garden, which includes a memorial to Siegel. Many guests wandering the gardens have reported seeing a man dressed in 1940s-style clothing walking along the winding paths. They have stated that he will glance over and flash a brilliant smile before he walks away and slowly vanishes before the startled guests can return his attentions.

Another area that has had many reports of Bugsy's spirit over the years is near the wedding chapel and the monument the hotel erected in honor of Siegel. This section of the gardens was where the original building was located and also where Bugsy's apartment stood. For four years before he was assassinated Siegel lived at the Flamingo resort. It was here he entertained his many guests and lady friends in the lap of luxury. Siegel had always dreamed of a life of ease, and at the Flamingo it seemed as if that dream had been reached. One couple who decided to go for a walk near the wedding chapel says that a man in an old-fashioned suit appeared in front of them and simply smiled, gave them a quick wink, and then disappeared. They said that he looked happy and in a pleasant mood and that his demeanor put them at ease rather than frightening them. They went on to say that if they had known that the man was the infamous Bugsy Siegel, they might not have been so calm.

Even though the hotel does not comment on any type of paranormal activity associated with the establishment, there have been plenty of employees who have told tales of Bugsy possibly haunting the hotel itself. The Presidential Suite of the new building is said to contain certain items from Bugsy's old apartment, most notable of these are the gold faucets that Bugsy himself picked out for his own bathroom. One evening when a guest had arrived back in the suite after a day of gambling, he heard what sounded like someone at the pool table. When he approached the table, however, he only caught a glimpse of a man before the specter vanished from sight, and he noticed that the pool table itself was completely undisturbed. Other guests have reported cold spots that seem to follow them around the suite, items that simply disappear only to reappear in another part of the room, and one of the maids watched as a glass rose off the kitchen counter and began floating around the room. The maid promptly quit after this incident.

Other guests of the hotel have seen a man in 1940s-style clothing standing by the pool, watching it would seem, the pretty girls in their bathing suits. For a ladies man like Siegel, the new suits must be a shock and a pleasure.

This monument to Bugsy in the gardens of the Flamingo Hotel is one of the places where Siegel's spirit is seen most often.

One of the interesting things about the reports of Bugsy Siegel's spirit from the Flamingo Hotel is that, no matter who is telling the tale, it would seem that he is happy being there. I guess we should not be surprised about this as the resort was his dream. He is most likely glad to see that his vision of what Las Vegas could become has turned out even better than he had hoped.

The Flamingo Hotel and Resort is not the only place Ben Siegel's ghost has been seen. The mansion once belonging to his girlfriend and the place he was brutally gunned down has a long history of his residual spirit. Almost all of the reports state that his ghost rises from the couch in a panic as he flees from a hail of bullets, yet he is always unsuccessful in avoiding his death. The way it is always described as the same scene repeated over and over indicates a residual haunting rather than an intelligent haunting. One psychic who investigated the home said that it was Siegel's imprint from the last, terrified moments of his life after he spotted his killer, that it is his fear, which left behind this spiritual video if you will, that has left its mark on the property. There is a problem with this theory, however. Bugsy Siegel never saw the bullets coming and never saw his assassin, and his first hint that his life was over came as the first bullet entered his skull. The crime scene photos even show the newspaper he was reading on the floor between his legs below his body, which is still slumped on the couch where he died.

Whether or not Bugsy's imprint is on the house where he was brutally gunned down or it is simply a case of wild imagination due to people knowing he was killed at the residence, one thing is for sure: Benjamin "Bugsy" Siegel has become more famous in death than he had been in life. You would be hard pressed to find anyone who has not heard of him, and the playboy gangster has appeared in numerous movies about the Mob, including Warren Beatty's portrayal of him in the movie about his life simply titled *Bugsy*.

Las Vegas has become a gambling Mecca due to Siegel, and he has now firmly become an American icon. I'm sure Bugsy would be pleased. So when you travel to Las Vegas for your next outing, stop by the world-famous Flamingo Resort and Casino and say hello to Mr. Siegel. I'm sure he'll have a smile and a wink waiting for you.

CHAPTER 5

GEORGE REEVES

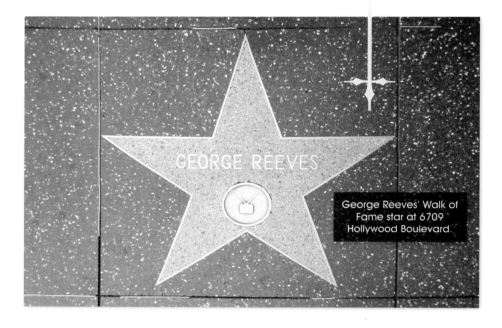

GEORGE REEVES

George Reeves' Walk of Fame star at 6709 Hollywood Boulevard.

Faster than a speeding bullet, more powerful than a
locomotive, able to leap tall buildings in a single bound...
Look, up in the sky!
IT'S A BIRD, IT'S A PLANE, IT'S...SUPERMAN.

We have all heard these words from the many movies and TV shows over the years; we all know who Superman is. For those old enough to remember, or for those that have seen the syndicated *Adventures of Superman* television show, the name George Reeves will be familiar as the first Superman on television. While kryptonite was the bane of the man from Krypton, Superman was the bane of George Reeves and may have led to him killing himself in 1959; there are those, however, who believe that Reeves was murdered. Could there have been a Lex Luthor hiding in Reeves's bedroom the night of his death as some claim, or was it depression that became the TV Superman's real kryptonite?

George Reeves was born George Keefer Brewer on January 5, 1914, in Woolstock, Iowa. He was born only five months into his parents' marriage, and his father, Don Brewer, left shortly after his birth. Unable to support herself and her young son, George's mother, Helen Lescher, moved back to her hometown of Galesburg, Illinois, to be close to her family who would help her raise George. Not content in Illinois, Helen moved again, this time to Pasadena, California, where she lived with her sister. Helen soon met and fell in love with Frank Bessolo, who adopted George and by all accounts became a great father to him. The marriage lasted fifteen years; while George was away visiting relatives, his mother divorced Frank and told her son that he had committed suicide. George believed his mother, and it would be years before he found out the truth of the matter: that the only man he knew as his father was still living.

George had always been an outgoing and open young man while growing up, and this led him to the stage while in high school. He would perform in every play and musical while in school, but he also found that he loved boxing even more than he loved acting. Reeves began to compete in amateur matches and worked his way up to the heavy-weight category. His mother would constantly worry that he was going to get injured and ruin his good looks. She repeatedly told him to stop competing, but Reeves was determined to pursue professional boxing after he graduated from college. He continued to act while attending Pasadena Junior College and began to try out for parts at the famed Pasadena Playhouse. As he gained more and more parts in this venue, his mother became more adamant about him giving up his dream of winning a boxing championship until Reeves finally relented to spare his mother any more heartache.

While performing at the Pasadena Playhouse, an agent working for various studios saw Reeves on stage and thought he would be perfect for a part in the soon-to-be-filmed *Gone With the Wind*. He was cast in the role of Stuart Tarlton, one of Scarlett O'Hara's suitors. When the film was released, the credits incorrectly listed Reeves as playing Brent Tarlton, portrayed by Fred Crane. This, however, did not take away from Reeves's outstanding job in the film or his incredible stage presence. Even though he played a minor role, Warner Brothers signed him to a contract soon after the movie was released. It was Warner who made him change his name from George Bessolo to George Reeves, thinking it sounded more "common man" and, therefore, more relatable to audiences. Reeves would go on to appear in two movies with Ronald Reagan and three with James Cagney before Warner loaned him out to Universal Studios.

After his contract with Warner Brothers expired, Reeves signed with 20th Century Fox but only appeared in a few films for them before being released. He then was cast in the Paramount war drama *So Proudly We Hail* with Claudette Colbert; this movie garnered rave reviews, but Reeves was drafted in early 1943, which put his film career on hold — at least his civilian career. While in the Army he was assigned to the Air Corps Broadway show *Winged Victory*, which was designed to sell war bonds. This was followed up by a national tour. George and his college sweetheart, Ellenora Needles, were married in 1940; they were now finding it hard to make ends meet on his Army pay, so a friend of the cast, Moss Hart, arranged for Reeves to take on an extra job in wardrobe. When Ellenora moved east to be with George, Moss got her a job as an understudy as well.

After the war bond tour and a short stint making a movie version of *Winged Victory*, George spent the remainder of the war starring in training films. When he was released from duty in 1946, Reeves returned to Hollywood but was having trouble finding film roles, so he again performed at the Pasadena Playhouse and took small parts in a couple of B-movie thrillers. In 1949, he was cast in the starring role of Sir Galahad in the serial *The Adventures of Sir Galahad*. George Reeves had a superb memory; this made him ideally suited to the fast-paced production schedule of a series. Unfortunately, the serial was cancelled after fifteen episodes, and with his pending divorce on the horizon, Reeves decided it was time for a change.

He moved to New York City in late 1949 where he took roles in live TV shows as well as performing in numerous radio broadcasts. His marriage was finally dissolved in 1950, but since there were no parts coming his way from Hollywood, he decided to remain in New York, continuing with the smaller roles that were flooding in for him. He finally returned home in 1951 when RKO Pictures asked him to appear in their film *Rancho Notorious,* with Marlene Dietrich, Arthur Kennedy, and Mel Farrer. In June of that same year, George Reeves signed a seven-year contract to star in the new television show *The Adventures of Superman.*

Toni Mannix purchased this home for
George along with his Jaguar.

Originally reluctant to start another serial or series, he finally agreed when they told him that the pilot would be shot as a feature film, albeit a B-movie, but a film nonetheless. Like most actors at that time, television was thought to be a flash in the pan and, therefore, "serious" actors would not be able to have their roles seen by many people if they performed on TV. George Reeves was no different; he wanted his work noticed by the audience and the movie executives. Production began on *Superman and the Mole Men* shortly after the contract was signed, and was released in November of that same year.

As soon as filming was completed on the film/pilot for the new series, production began in earnest. The full season of shows, twenty-four in all, were shot over a period of thirteen weeks: To save money, four or more shows were shot at the same time if the same set was used for each show. This mixing of scripts was confusing for many of the actors, but Reeves's memory for dialog made him almost infallible in shooting these scenes. *The Adventures of Superman* made its television premiere on September 19, 1952, on WENR-TV in Chicago.

All of the cast members of the show had restrictions on their contracts, which forbade them from taking any other jobs that could interfere with the show's filming schedule. Their salaries were not great, and many of them complained about this restriction. Reeves, being the star of the show and having a huge fan base because of it, was able to make quite a bit of extra money in personal appearances. George loved his younger fans and was always careful to keep his clean-cut image whenever he was around them—as a role model, he felt it was his duty to the children. He was well liked on the set; known as a jokester, Reeves was always playing tricks on his fellow cast and crew. All were in good fun, and everyone enjoyed them. One crew member said: "Mr. Reeves would always have this grin on his face, which made you wonder if you were next to get pranked; it was fun and scary but made the days go by much faster and with much more fun."

Not content with just being Superman, Reeves was still trying out for movie roles; in 1953, he appeared in two feature films, *Forever Female,* with Ginger Rodgers and William Holden, and *The Blue Gardenia,* staring Anne Baxter and Raymond Burr. Even with these film credits to his name he had become so closely associated with the Man of Steel that he was having problems finding other roles. Once season two was done shooting, he became so dissatisfied with the role and the low salary he decided to quit. He was now forty years old and needed to get his film career back on track. Reeves started up his own production company, wrote a script for his original new TV series *Port of Entry,* and was just in the process of seeking out financial backing for the show when the producers of *The Adventures of Superman* offered him a substantial raise if he would come back to the show; $5,000 a week was an offer he couldn't refuse.

It was right around this time that he began his affair with Toni Mannix, the wife of MGM General Manager Eddie Mannix. Toni was eight years Reeves' senior, and the affair was not only known to Toni's husband, but was approved of by him as well. The Superman star was often seen at the Mannix home, and friends have said that he would walk in while the couple was having breakfast, fix himself a bowl of cereal, sit down with them, and eat and chat until Toni was ready to leave for the day with him. It was Mannix who purchased the home on Benedict Canyon Drive and the car George drove. Reeves would break up with her in 1959, just five months before his death.

Still unhappy about his inability to separate himself from his TV character, Reeves tried to showcase his versatility as a performer, and to that end, he appeared on *The Tony Bennett Show* in August of 1956—he sang for the audience. Then he went on the *I Love Lucy* program as Superman to let people know of his comedic abilities. This led to him being cast in the Disney Studios production of *Westward Ho, the Wagons!* This would be George Reeves's final feature film. From 1957 until his death, Reeves, Noel Neill, Natividad Vacio, and Gene LeBell would perform a Superman sketch for live audiences, and Reeves would play guitar and sing to the delight of the crowds.

George Reeves had always had a problem with depression; he kept it in check with medication and periodic visits to psychiatrists when it hit hard. This may be one of the reasons George had always been known as a bad boy and a hard drinking partier. This was a coping mechanism that may have helped him deal with the downtimes in his life. As 1959 dawned, he had announced his engagement to Leonore Lemmon. The producers of *Superman* had announced that a new, revamped season of the show had been ordered and a new stage show of *Superman* had been scheduled with a tour in Australia. Everything seemed to be going his way. Reeves may not have seen things this way, however. At the age of forty-five, beginning a new year as Superman was not something he really wanted to do; he still longed for prominent movie roles, still wanted to start his own production company, and direct his own films. To him, Superman was holding him back. He had complained to his mother that finances were tight, and that was the only reason he had agreed to continue on as the Man of Steel. It was strictly for the money.

On the night of June 15, 1959, George Reeves, Leonore Lemmon, and writer Richard Condon were at a local restaurant eating, drinking, and enjoying a night out when Lemmon and Reeves got into an argument, and the three left and went home. By the time they arrived, the couple was back on good terms, and the three spent the rest of the evening drinking in the living room until Reeves went upstairs to bed. Sometime around midnight the doorbell rang. Lemmon answered the door to find a drunk William Bliss with their neighbor Carol Van Ronkel wanting to come in and have an impromptu party. Being drunk herself by this time, Leonore was more than happy to oblige. Even though George Reeves had a reputation for loving to party, everyone knew that he did not allow guests at his house after midnight. This night, however, they ignored his wishes and were getting quite loud, which woke him up from a deep sleep. He then came downstairs and confronted the group, telling them that they all had to leave. Lemmon then waded into the confrontation telling Reeves that he was being rude, that they were guests of hers, and that she didn't want them to leave. After a brief argument with his fiancé, George calmed down a bit, had a drink, and then went back upstairs—still in a bad mood. A few minutes later, a single gunshot was heard, and George Reeves was dead.

It would seem that TV's Superman had succumbed to his depression and had taken his own life. All the statements from the people at the house that night are the same and corroborate the official cause of death as that of suicide. However, some things may not be as they seem on the surface. The official story has the guests hearing the gunshot with Bliss rushing to the bedroom to find Reeves lying across the bed, naked, his feet on the floor with a single wound from his own .30 cal. Luger to the side of his head. It then took them a little over an hour to call the police. They claimed that their inebriation, the late hour, and the shock of what had happened caused confusion and grief, and this was the reason for their delay in calling.

The police report says that the state of intoxication of the witnesses made it extremely hard to get "coherent stories." Some of the statements had Lemmon as the one who found the body, others that it was Bliss, and still another that they all rushed to the room to see what had happened. One of the odd things to come out, and one that was reported in the newspapers after the event, said that as Reeves retired to his room, Lemmon was heard saying, "He's probably going to go shoot himself." After a noise was heard upstairs, she said, "There, he's opening the drawer to the gun," and then after the shot rang out, she blurted, "See there? I told you so." Lemmon told the police that she wasn't surprised that he took his own life as he was extremely depressed by his failed career.

Even though Lemmon and the rest of the guests at the house that night told the police that Bliss is the one who went upstairs while the rest of the party remained in the living room, a friend of Reeves, who also knew Bill Bliss's wife's best friend was told that Bill admitted that Lemmon was upstairs with George when the gunshot rang out; shortly thereafter, Lemmon came rushing down frantically saying, "Tell them I was down here; tell them I was down here." If this is true, then Lemmon may have been the one to pull the trigger, or at the very least may have witnessed what actually occurred.

During the police investigation of Reeves' death, both Lemmon and Mannix became possible suspects in the murder of Reeves. In the case of Leonore Lemmon, it was determined that even though there were discrepancies with her statements and those of the other guests, there was just no motive. This was not the case for Toni Mannix, however. The police surmised that because of the break up with Reeves five months earlier, and that she had purchased the home he lived in along with the Jaguar he drove, the loss of his affection had hit her hard. It was also known that her husband had connections with organized crime and that he also was upset that Reeves had broken his wife's heart and had, therefore, used those connections to have Reeves killed. The theory goes that either Toni herself or a hired gun waited in Reeves' room for him to return, shot him with his own gun (Toni knew where George kept the Luger), and then escaped out the front bedroom window to a waiting car. This was thought to have been a last resort after several failed attempts, one being the possible draining of the brake fluid from his car and another being a collision with a delivery truck, both of which occurred in the last months of Reeves' life. Even with all of the suspicions of possible murder, the official cause of death was ruled, "suicide by a single gunshot wound to the head."

PARANORMAL ASSOCIATION

There are many today who simply refuse to believe that George Reeves would have committed suicide. He had just signed on for another revamped season of *Superman*, had an exhibition fight with Archie Manning coming up that he was looking forward to, and was about to be married to the woman he loved. So why would he take his own life? There are stories that leading up to the day of his death, other attempts on his life took place, which would lead one to believe in the murder theory. But if you take into account his long battle with depression, it is not hard to understand that he may have decided to end his existence. The confusion surrounding his death will most likely never be cleared up, and all of the questions about suicide, murder, or accident may be the reason that George Reeves has refused to pass into the light and move on.

After Reeves' death, his house reverted back to the woman who bought it for him, and one of the main suspects in his possible murder, Toni Mannix. Mannix had been in love with George, and since this was all she had left of him, she was loath to sell the property, deciding to rent it out instead. Mannix soon found that no matter how many times she rented the house, the tenants wouldn't stay for long. When asked why they were moving out, they would say that, "The noises in the upstairs room wouldn't stop," or "We kept hearing a gun shot."

One couple who rented the house told how they were hosting a party when they heard a loud commotion coming from the upstairs room. Thinking that the house was being broken into, a few of the men went up to the bedroom, the room where Reeves was found dead, only to find the room in a complete shambles. "It looked like someone had turned a tornado loose" is how one of the guests described the scene. Others have reported things being moved around, such as drinks turning up in the kitchen when they had been left in the living room or dining room. One couple had

George Reeves' spirit is often seen standing at these windows in full Superman costume.

a German shepard who approached the bedroom door and wouldn't stop barking; it was almost as if the dog sensed something behind the door that scared it. The barking continued for a few minutes, and then the dog let out a whimper and ran away with its tail between its legs. The couple opened the door and discovered that their bed had been moved from one side of the room to the other and that the room itself was a mess, even though it had been orderly when they had left it.

Over the years, the house has seen many tenants and owners come and go. In every case they say they are leaving because they just can't stand to live in the house with its strange occurrences. All of the tales are similar: They keep hearing a single gun shot late at night, which wakes them up. Those sleeping in the bedroom where Reeves died say that the shot they hear is coming from inside the room; others claim that the smell of gunpowder is sometimes so overwhelming that they have to leave the house. They all claim that no matter how well kept and orderly the bedroom is, they will come back to find it completely disheveled with the bed moved, drawers open and empty with the clothes from the drawers strewn about the room, as well as the contents of the closet a total mess. One couple living in the home and using Reeves' bedroom, say that they woke up one night around 2 a.m. to find Reeves standing over them in his classic Superman pose wearing his costume, replete with cape. As they watched, Reeves turned towards them, gave them that boyish grin he used so well, and then simply vanished. They immediately packed their belongings and moved out.

Reeves, even though he wanted out of the *Superman* rut he had found himself in when he was alive, seems to have embraced it after his death. Many times he has been seen wearing his costume; both owners of the house and renters have reported seeing him in and around the house wearing his getup. Once the police were called to the house by a neighbor who told them that Superman was in the front yard of the home. Of course, by the time they arrived the apparition was nowhere to be found, and the police just chalked it up to hysteria. Another time when the house was being used as a film location, Reeves decided to make an appearance in the middle of shooting a scene; he was seen by quite a few actors and crew—again, he was in full costume and stood there a few seconds before vanishing.

Perhaps the strangest case involving the home took place when the Los Angeles Sheriff's Department received a call from neighbors who had heard gunshots and screaming coming from the house. The police responded, and even though nothing out of the ordinary was found, a unit was told to stay behind and keep a watch on the place for the rest of the evening. No official report was made of what happened next, but from what was gathered from the officers, they saw the ghost of George Reeves standing on the roof of the house as Superman, who then vanished only to reappear directly in front of their car. The officers promptly drove off.

Another possible place that Reeves may haunt is the Pasadena Playhouse. It is not in dispute that the theater is haunted; however, those in the know say that it could be Reeves and/or the former founder, Gilmore Brown. There are those who say the haunts of the playhouse go back a year before Gilmore's death, which coincides with the timeline of Reeves's death the year prior. The spirit of the Pasadena Playhouse has always been known as a prankster, and although Gilmore was never really known for that in life, George Reeves was well know for his love of playing jokes on his friends and co-workers—which is exactly what happens at the playhouse. It is also well known that Reeves thought of the theater as his home away from home, which could be one of the reasons his spirit may linger here. I will not debate the merits one way or another in these pages; I merely put it forth as a possibility for those interested.

George Reeves's death will always be shrouded in mystery: Was it just a case of accidental suicide, blatant suicide, or cold-blooded murder? In the movie *Hollywoodland,* they end the show with alternate endings to reflect the whole host of possibilities, leaving the viewer to decide what the truth is. It is the same in the actual life of Reeves: Each person must decide the truth of his ending as the one they wish to believe. What is true on the whole, however, is that George Reeves, as successful as he was, wanted and needed more in his life from Hollywood, and his inability to gain that which he thought should be his may have been the catalyst for him to end his life way too soon. As the Introduction to his *Superman* TV show says, George Reeves's life was, "faster than a speeding bullet."

George Bessolo Reeves' ashes at Mountain View Cemetery near Hollywood.

CHAPTER 6

THE LOS FELIZ MURDER MANSION

The graves of Lillian and Dr. Harold Perelson.

Family is about love, caring, and nurturing. You marry because of the love you feel for your wife or husband; when you have children that love is spread to them, and your life is now devoted to the raising and nurturing of those children. In turn, the lessons you teach them will be handed down to the next generation, and so on down the line. What happens when the lessons learned are those of murder and madness, when the last thing the children remember of their parents is of death and betrayal? What have you handed down when your kids see their mother dead and their father covered in her blood and coming for them? These and other questions still remain unanswered in one of the most bizarre cases in Los Angeles history, as well as the strange aftermath that still haunts Los Feliz today.

Doctor Harold Perelson was a prominent surgeon specializing in cardiothoracics and allergies. He had gained a successful and profitable patent, in 1941, for a new type of syringe, had written one of the most respected clinical reports of the time—the electrocardiogram in familial periodic paralysis, which was featured in the magazine, *American Heart Journal*, in June 1949—and was a well respected keynote speaker in medical conferences all around the country. Perelson was an assistant head of Cardiology for the School of Medicine at the University of Southern California, Los Angeles, and was on the surgical teams of cardiology at Los Angeles County General, Cedars of Lebanon Hospital, and the Santa Fe Hospital of Los Angeles. Dr. Perelson's life, by all accounts, was a storybook life of wealth, fame, and unmitigated success. So why then would Perelson decide to kill his family and himself?

On the night of December 6, 1959, Harold Perelson came home from work, greeted his wife and kids, fixed himself a drink, and casually watched his wife wrap Christmas presents while she waited for dinner to be ready. Even though they were Jewish, the Perelsons had begun celebrating the holiday with their friends and co-workers and enjoyed the sense of community it imparted on their family. His wife, Lillian, was a wonderful mother and homemaker and called the family together for dinner at the table where they sat eating and talking about their week at work and school. Their eighteen-year-old daughter, Judye, talked about her friends and the boys she liked; the whole scene was right out of a Rockwell painting.

After dinner, the family stayed up to watch a bit of television, and then Lillian and Harold tucked their eleven-year-old daughter, Debbie, and thirteen-year-old son, Joseph, into bed. Judye went to her room to work on some homework while her mother went to the master bedroom to read. Harold remained downstairs until he knew his wife was asleep and then went upstairs to read his copy of Dante's *Divine Comedy* until he himself fell asleep right after marking a passage he found personally compelling.

Sometime around 5 a.m., Dr. Perelson awoke, placed the book he had been reading on the nightstand and went down to the kitchen where he kept a small tool chest. He retrieved a ball peen hammer, casually walked back to his bedroom where he approached the bed where his wife was sleeping soundly. He stood gazing down at her for a minute and then raised the hammer . . . and in one swift motion, he brought the hammer crashing down on Lillian's head and then again and again until it was a bloody mess. Perelson then left the room and walked into his daughter Judye's bedroom and began to attack her with the hammer. Judye had already been awakened by the sound of her mother being murdered, and this most likely saved her life. As the hammer came down towards her skull she just managed to get her arm up, which softened the initial blow. The weapon still connected with her head, however, and the force of the hit disoriented her as she tried to get up and away from her rampaging father. As Judye saw the first swing of the hammer, she had let out a blood-curdling scream. This not only awoke the neighbors nearby but her sleeping siblings as well. Perelson heard his youngest daughter emerging from her bedroom and, thinking his oldest was incapacitated, casually left Judye's room to see to his youngest child. Perelson walked Debbie back to her room and told her, "Go back to bed baby; this is just a nightmare." He then proceeded back to Judye's bedroom.

While Dr. Perelson had been busy with his other daughter, Judye had regained some of her senses and had fled the house; she made her way to the neighbors, who, already awakened from her screams, quickly came to the door. The neighbor, seeing the blood streaming from the young girl's head immediately notified police who called for an ambulance and sent patrol cars to the scene. Meanwhile, Debbie, who had not believed her father that she had been dreaming, gathered up her brother and they too fled from the house before Perelson could use the ball peen hammer on them as well. The doctor, knowing full well that the police must be on the way to his house, went back upstairs, got a bottle of pills from the medicine cabinet, sat down on the bed, and took all of the pills in a single gulp. (Most of the reports from around the Internet claim that he drank a glass of acid to kill himself. I could find no truth of this actually occurring and believe this is just an attempt to make the story more bizarre. All of the newspaper accounts from the day state that he overdosed on pills.)

When the police arrived at the house, they first went to speak with the neighbors and the children to make sure they were okay. Judye was immediately sent by ambulance to the hospital with a fracture to the skull and severe bruising; Judye would survive with no lingering physical injuries. As the officers approached the door, another neighbor informed them that he had been knocking but had gotten no response from anyone inside. They carefully entered the home and called out to Perelson, but were met with silence. They went upstairs and found Harold Perelson lying on the floor in his bedroom, the ball peen hammer in his hand and an empty pill bottle next to him. His wife, Lillian, was in the bed, her head fractured so badly that she was unrecognizable; blood was splattered all over the wall behind her, and the bed linens were soaked with her blood. On the nightstand next to Harold's side of the bed, the book by Dante that he had been reading was still open to Canto 1; it read, "Midway upon the journey of our life I found myself within a forest dark, for the straightforward pathway had been lost…"

Lillian Perelson was brutally murdered by her husband with a ball-peen hammer.

The investigation into the events of that morning were pretty straightforward. It was obvious by the scene of the crime and the statements of the children and neighbors that Dr. Perelson had murdered his wife, attempted to murder his oldest daughter, and had then killed himself by overdose. What wasn't clear, however, was why. All of the neighbors said the same thing: The Perelson's were a loving family and showed no outward signs of strife. When the police made a routine of Judye's car ,they found a letter she had written to her aunt that said, "We are on the merry-go-round again, same problems, same worries, only tenfold. My parents are in a bind financially." The letter then went on to say how she would be looking for a job to be able to help the family through this crisis. It is believed by some that Perelson had finally snapped under the pressures of his finances and had decided that the death of his family was preferable to living with worry and in poverty. It is conceivable that if his attempt to kill Judye had been successful, he would have then attempted to kill his younger children. We will never know what had been going through his mind that fateful morning, but as tragic as the death of his wife and his suicide were, it could have been much worse.

After the furor had died down and the press no longer deemed the events of that night newsworthy, the mansion was sold at auction with the proceeds going to settle the estate's debts, and the remainder going to the children. The couple who purchased the home, Julian and Emily Enriquez, only visited the home on rare occasions and used it for storing items that they didn't want in their home; in effect, they bought the mansion to be used as a storage shed of sorts. Over the years, they would visit the house to either bring something new into this storage site or to remove an item. They were never overly friendly with the neighbors, nor were they rude or unwelcoming—they were just . . . there.

When Julian and Emily passed away in 1994, ownership of the mansion passed to their son, Rudy. Most of the neighbors expected the house to finally be renovated and either sold to a new family, rented out, or they figured Rudy would move in himself. Unfortunately, none of those things happened; Rudy continued to use the house as storage. The neighbors complained to the city that the home was being used as a squatter's hangout; other times they told how prostitutes would come in and use the home for entertaining their "tricks." Slowly the house and property began to decline; the neighbors began to clean up the outside yard and would tidy up the curbside, but the house itself was declining. And even though Rudy had installed an alarm system to alert the police if anyone entered the house, the backyard was still being used as a homeless camp. Then came the ghost hunters.

The story of the murder had been widely told, and when, in 2009, the *Los Angeles Times* wrote an article on the house and mentioned the possibility of it being haunted, the flood gates were opened. One of the stories in the *Times* article mentioned how the Enriquez family bought the mansion but never removed the Perelson's furniture. Not only were the furnishings the same as when the children fled the home, but everything was still the exact same as the night of the murder; this included the wrapping paper that Lillian had been using for the Christmas presents and the tree itself was still standing in the living room near the 1950s television set. Family board games were still stacked neatly where they had been left, and in the laundry room, clothes were still hung out to dry. In the kitchen, cleaning supplies were where they had been left, and a case of SpaghettiOs was still on the counter. Since the article was released, many photos of the inside of the house have made their way to the Internet and have confirmed all of these reports.

The house is now falling apart; there are "no trespassing" signs out front and along the back fence. The windows are so dirty that it is hard to see into the home, and the front door shows signs of many break-in attempts. At one point, the city contacted the owner and demanded that he repair the roof, or they would be forced to condemn the property. The grounds are laced with gopher holes; the once-beautiful fountain is now dry except when it rains, and weeds have taken over where once a lovely garden stood. It is truly a sad sight when one thinks about how beautiful this Spanish-style, three-story mansion, built in 1925, must have looked in its heyday.

The mansion where all of the furnishings, decorations, and foodstuffs are still the same as the night the gruesome attacks took place.

PARANORMAL ASSOCIATION

Empty houses seem to always get the moniker of haunted, especially when a gruesome murder has occurred within its wall. The Los Feliz Murder Mansion, as it is called, is no different; in fact, this home was considered haunted almost before the blood-soaked sheets had dried in the bedroom. In 2009, the *Los Angeles Times* wrote a story about the house and the mystery surrounding it; in the article they mention the possibility of the mansion being haunted even though the current owner, Rudy Enriquez, himself disputes it. However, Mr. Enriquez only goes to the property to feed a couple of cats he keeps at the house. Residents feel differently. In the *Times* piece, it tells the tale of a neighbor's friend who had a "Nancy Drew moment", and opened a back door to enter the house; she didn't get far, however, as a burglar alarm went off, and she promptly left. The story goes on to say about the friend, "Two nights later, the alarm kept going off at my house on my back door, but there was no one there. It was like the ghost was following us." Since that story in the *Times,* ghost hunters have been flocking to the mansion in the hopes of getting proof of the afterlife.

Paranormal investigators have always been a vocal group; they like to boast about their discoveries and evidence, real or imagined, and many of these have spoken of hearing voices and whispers while roaming the outside of the house. One of these swears that he has felt the presence of extreme evil permeating the very walls of the home. Many of the tales, including those of evil and demons must be taken with a grain of salt; however, some of the tales may be valid.

Orbs are one of those things that this author finds dubious at best, but many have been photographed within the home through the windows. What makes this a bit more compelling for us non-orb believers, is wondering what has stirred up the dust that is usually the cause of most orb activity, in an empty house — one, I might add, that has been empty of all human traffic for years. It is true that wind may be getting into the house through leaky windows, but there does seem to be an over abundance of this within the home's walls. Another common occurrence seems to be the sounds of screams and moans being heard by intrepid ghost hunters in the wee morning hours. The hunters have reported hearing the sound of a woman calling out "No!" in a terrified voice followed by her frantic screaming and then silence. This silence is then shortly followed by the low moan of a male, who sounds as if he is in distress; this moaning goes on for a short while until all is again silent. Could this be the sound of Harold killing his wife and then his sorrowful moans once he has realized what he has done?

What would possess Dr. Perelson to attack and kill
his wife and then commit suicide?

Perhaps the most reported events coming from these ghost hunters are the sightings of faces that stare out of the windows of the old mansion. I have heard this from many individuals who have been to the property, and the tales seem to all be the same. The hunters tell of seeing the face of a woman staring at them through one of the upstairs windows; she will gaze at them for a few minutes and then simply vanish from sight. Many have photographed this apparition, but when they got home and downloaded the photos onto their computers or got their film developed she was not in any of the frames—it is as if she wants to make herself known but does not like the camera. The neighbors who live near the mansion have reported no activity to speak of; this could be because they fear their quiet street may become even busier than it has since the *LA Times* article came out, or it may be because they have seen none of the reported activity that the ghost hunters claim to have seen. Whatever the case, the story of the house is odd enough.

Judye, Debbie, and Joseph survived their father's apparent insanity, and once they had been sent east to live with relatives, they vanished from sight. It is believed that their names were changed in an attempt to protect them from the notoriety that followed, and it seems to have worked. Why Dr. Perelson committed this crime is still a mystery, and unless one of the lost Perelson children decide to break their long silence, it seems we will never truly know. Rumor has it that his wife had him committed, and once he was released, he killed her. Again this is a tale that may or may not be true, but whatever the reason, it is truly a sad story and one of the oddest ones concerning a marvelous mansion abandoned in time and memory.

CHAPTER 7
MARILYN MONROE

Marilyn Monroe's Walk of Fame star at 6774 Hollywood Boulevard.

Marilyn Monroe. Just say the name and images of sex appeal, blond hair, beauty, and vapidity all flood into a person's mind. The trouble is that Norma Jean Baker was much more than that, more than her Hollywood persona, and more than what history has written about her. Beautiful, yes, but she was an intelligent woman who wanted control of her life and took it, even as it spiraled out of control because of the lost little girl inside and her fears that she could never seem to get away from no matter how far she ran. The myth surrounding her in life, grown to monstrous size in death, has defined a woman whose only crime was that of desperately needing love and turning it into a dark fairy tale that no longer resembled the truth of the woman, or of the life that she led and the life she so desperately coveted. Marilyn died at the young age of thirty-six, and the legends, mostly bad, that have sprung up regarding her troubled life may be the reason that this beautiful woman has never been able to find peace in the afterlife. Marilyn once said that, "Men don't see me; they just lay their eyes on me." Maybe, just maybe, if we can all come to actually see Norma Jean for who she was, Marilyn can finally pass on into the light and finally find love.

Born Norma Jean Mortenson on June 1, 1926, Marilyn Monroe had anything but a normal childhood. Norma's mother, Gladys, would spend her entire life in and out of mental hospitals, and having very little to no family to rely on meant young Norma would spend her childhood bouncing around from one foster home to another, including at least one orphanage, until she was old enough to be on her own. Shortly after Norma's birth, Gladys sent her to live with a devout Christian Science religious couple from Gladys's church, Ida and Albert Bolender. Gladys had found full-time work but had no time for Norma and so paid the Bolenders twenty-five dollars a month to look after her daughter. Norma spent seven years with the Bolenders until the couple decided to move back to their home country of England; they offered to adopt Norma but Gladys, back in a mental institution, refused to grant them the request. During the time Norma was with the Bolenders, they were the only family she knew; Marilyn said she remembered a time when she called Ida, "mommy," and Ida responded back with anger saying, "Don't you ever call me mother; I'm not your mother." Marilyn goes on to recall asking Ida if Albert was her father and again got an angry, "no." What a devastating and confusing time that must have been for that poor sweet girl.

Gladys, knowing that she had to do something, used what little money she had accumulated in her various jobs to purchase a small house near the Hollywood Bowl and brought Norma home to live with her. Unfortunately, this didn't last, and Norma's mother reentered an asylum, leaving Norma Jean again to fend for herself. The young girl spent a few years moving from one foster home to another with brief stints living in Gladys's small house until Grace McKee stepped in and took custody of Norma. Grace had been a friend of her mother's for some time and felt obligated to care for the child after she had signed papers committing Gladys to yet another insane asylum. Norma lived with Grace only a short time before Grace met and married Ervin Goddard. Ervin was not overly fond of Norma Jean, and when he brought one of his own daughters from a previous marriage home to live with them, Norma was sent to the Los Angeles Orphans Home. Norma Jean lived in the orphanage for two years before Grace came to bring her back to live with them. Norma had only been there a couple of months when, one night, Ervin snuck into the young girl's room and molested her. Grace blamed Norma for the incident and sent her away to live with her uncle's mother, Olive Brunings. Norma lived with Brunings for a year, and then, in August of 1938, at the age of twelve, Norma Jean was sexually assaulted again, this time by one of Brunings's sons; she was immediately sent back to the Goddards, who then sent her to live with Grace's aunt, Ana Lower. While living with Lower, Norma Jean was taken to weekly Christian Science services and was pushed to accept the religion as her own. Norma had grown up in the faith and now began to question it. In her mind, everyone involved with the religion, including her mother, had molested her, blamed her, or abandoned her; the fact that another person, who was not her family, was again pushing it down her throat only made her beliefs more confusing.

Lower died in late 1940, and Norma was again passed back to Grace and Ervin Goddard. In 1941, Norma met and began seeing the boy next door, James Dougherty; they were just friends as Jim was five years her senior, but Norma Jean had already blossomed into a stunning, beautiful young woman, and it had not gone unnoticed by Jim or any of the other boys in Norma's high school. She already had a following of admirers and Grace knew that it could spell trouble. In 1942, Ervin Goddard's job was relocated to West Virginia, but because Norma was not their child and no papers had ever been filed giving them legal custody of Norma Jean, they could not take her out of state, which meant that Norma faced the real possibility of returning to an orphanage.

There is much disagreement among historians on whether Grace went behind Norma's back to arrange the marriage or if Norma herself had agreed to marry Jim Dougherty, but in either case, just after Norma Jean Baker's sixteenth birthday, she became Norma Jean Dougherty. Norma no longer had to worry about going to an orphanage, but she did have to worry about being a wife to her twenty-one-year-old husband. Just after their nuptials, Norma dropped out of high school and tried to settle into her role as a housewife.

Jim had been working at the Lockheed Aircraft factory in Southern California, and the boredom of married life, staying home waiting for her husband to return from work, cleaning, and cooking day after day was wearing on Norma. In 1943, Jim enlisted in the Merchant Marines, and when he was sent to Catalina Island, just off the coast of California, Norma Jean went with him. She loved living there; she had the same homemaker tasks that she'd performed on the mainland, but now, when she was done with her tasks, instead of sitting down with a magazine or book, she would go to the beach, or to the small town of Avalon and explore the quaint tourist shops, or explore the coast for seashells or other decorative items to adorn their small cottage. She still wasn't happy with married life, but at least now it was livable. In April 1944, Jim shipped out to the Pacific war, and Norma was sent to live with his parents. Back on the mainland, Norma was no longer required to keep house, and wanting to help the war effort, she found a job at the Radioplane Munitions Factory.

With the war still raging, the US Army wanted to boost morale, and one of the ways they went about the task was to produce positive, uplifting films showing the home front and all of the progress the country was making in war materiel. In late 1944, the army sent a photographer to the Radioplane factory to take photos of the female workers; as soon as David Conover started snapping pictures of Norma Jean, he knew he had found someone special who was a natural in front of the camera. Conover shot many rolls with Norma as his subject while at the factory, and even though the army didn't use any of her photos, Conover convinced the young woman to quit her job and begin a career in modeling.

The Hollywood Roosevelt Hotel where Marilyn stayed once she made it big and where her ghost is often seen.

Norma went to work with Conover and his friends in January 1945 and shortly thereafter, at the urging and with the help of Conover, signed a contract with the Blue Book Model Agency in August of that same year. Blue Book started her out doing fashion shoots but soon took notice of her voluptuous figure, and she quickly became a pin-up star. By the spring of 1946, Norma Jean Dougherty had appeared on thirty-three magazine covers and was, "one of the agency's most ambitious and hard-working models." In June 1946, Norma had branched out into acting, and with the help of Emmeline Snively, the head of Blue Book, met Ben Lyon of 20th Century Fox, who gave her a screen test. Norma's screen test was nothing to write home about but adequate enough for the studio to give her a standard, six-month contract. In August, Norma Jean signed her first movie contract and then, in September, divorced Jim by sending him papers while he was on duty in China. Fox didn't think that Norma Jean was a name that would catch on to movie-going audiences, and in a compromise with the studio, allowed her name to be changed with Lyon picking the name Marilyn, after Broadway star Marilyn Miller and Norma demanding to use her mothers maiden name of Monroe, thus Marilyn Monroe was born.

During her first contract period, Marilyn was given no parts, so she spent time at the studio watching how films were made and observing other actors and actresses. Her contract was renewed in February, and a month later, she was cast in two films, *Dangerous Years* and the comedy *Scudda Hoo! Scudda Hay!* She only had ten lines of dialogue, but at last Marilyn had been seen in a movie. Fox did not renew her contract after the last film shoot, so Norma Jean went back to Blue Book and modeling. She also took acting classes and performed in small, local theater productions. She kept promoting herself to the various movie studios and, in 1948, signed a contract with Columbia Pictures. It is here that the transformation from Norma Jean Baker to screen legend Marilyn Monroe began. Monroe began working with Natasha Lytess, who was the studio's main drama coach. Lytess became Marilyn's mentor and had Marilyn make some changes to her appearance, namely bleaching her hair and raising her hairline. Marilyn Monroe made only one film while at Columbia—a low-budget, unsuccessful musical, but the important thing about the movie was that it was her first starring role. During her time at Columbia, she began dating her vocal coach, Fred Karger; it is rumored that he paid to have a slight overbite corrected, which actually helped her while singing in the film. Unfortunately, Columbia Pictures, like Fox, decided not to renew her contract, and again Norma Jean was back to square one.

In September 1948, Marilyn Monroe signed with the William Morris Agency and began a relationship with their vice-president, Johnny Hyde. Hyde fell in love with Monroe, but no matter how many times he proposed marriage, she always refused. Hyde personally began representing Monroe and, in what was at the time an untested and dangerous practice, paid for Marilyn to get minor plastic surgery. At the behest of Hyde, she was given a bit part in a Marx Brothers film and, to make ends meet, was still modeling. In May 1949, she posed nude for a calendar; this photo shoot by Tom Kelley would come back later to cause trouble, but at the time, it helped pay her bills.

With the help of Hyde and his agency, Monroe appeared in six films in 1950: two of the films were *The Asphalt Jungle* and *All About Eve*. Her portrayal of Angela in *The Asphalt Jungle* got her noticed, and this led to Hyde being able to negotiate a seven-year contract with 20th Century Fox in December of that year. A few days after Marilyn signed the contract with Fox, Hyde had a massive heart attack and died. Marilyn was heartbroken; even though she had refused to marry Johnny, she was very much in love with him. This was the beginning of a string of tragic events that would unfold in Norma Jean's life. During 1951, which was a breakout year for Marilyn, she would appear in four low budget films, one MGM drama, and three Fox comedies, as well as being a presenter in the 23rd Academy Awards. She received some good reviews from many critics and was receiving a lot of fan mail, but as one critic put it, "She was essentially a sexy ornament." As if to verify that comment she was declared "Miss Cheesecake of 1951" by the army newspaper *Stars and Stripes*. Monroe also had a series of relationships during that year, most notably with directors Elia Kazan and Nicholas Ray and with actors Peter Lawford and Yul Brynner; it would seem that Marilyn was looking for something she couldn't quite grasp.

In 1952, her second year with Fox, Marilyn finally broke out as a leading lady in two films. She received high acclaim for her role as a cannery worker in the film *Clash by Night*. These allowed her to showcase her acting range in both a comedy and a thriller; the films were commercial successes if not Academy-worthy films. Her name was getting out in the tabloids with Hedda Hopper and Florabel Muir giving her great reviews. It was during this time that the nude photos of Norma Jean came out to the public, and there was a mad scramble by both Marilyn and the studio to do damage control. It was decided to be up front with the brewing scandal, and Marilyn gave a series of interviews explaining that she had been in dire financial stress, and it was the only way for her to stay out of the poor house. This not only kept the gossip at a minimum, but a growing sympathy for Marilyn made the public even more willing to spend money on her films. This was also the year that Marilyn met the man who would become the love of her life: Joe DiMaggio.

In 1953, when the film *Niagara* was released, Monroe's performance caused an uproar with quite a few women's clubs who protested the film as "immoral." It received lukewarm reviews with words such as "morbid" and "clichéd" being used often. The one thing the film did do was to cement Marilyn's image as a sex symbol. Marilyn played up this new caricature of herself by wearing revealing outfits in public culminating in a most provocative dress while attending the *Photoplay* awards; this prompted actress Joan Crawford to say that her behavior was, "unbecoming an actress and a lady." Monroe didn't care as she knew it would further her career.

Marilyn Monroe was now making a lot of money for 20th Century Fox, but she was still not being paid as well as other star actresses who were bringing in as much – or less – than she was at the box office. In the movie *Gentlemen Prefer Blondes*, Monroe was making only $15,000 while her co-star, Jane Russell, made $200,000; this lack of respect would haunt Marilyn the rest of her life. The film made Marilyn a household name and also established her image as a "dumb blonde," which was anything but the truth. As part of the promotion for the film, Jane Russell and Marilyn Monroe were filmed pressing their hands and feet into wet cement at Grauman's Chinese Theater in what has now become one of the most famous clips in Hollywood history. In December 1953, Marilyn was featured on the cover of the first issue of *Playboy* and was also the first centerfold of the magazine; the photo used was one of her 1949 nude shots from her calendar photo shoot.

Marilyn Monroe's handprints at
Grauman's Chinese Theater.

Marilyn Monroe had become one of 20th Century Fox's biggest stars, but her contract still would not allow her to choose her projects or her co-stars, and her attempts at renegotiating with the studio had gone nowhere. Because of this, Marilyn refused to begin shooting on the next film Fox had chosen for her, another musical comedy with Frank Sinatra as co-star; this caused the studio to suspend Monroe on January 4, 1954. In an effort to counter the negative publicity, Marilyn went to the press to strengthen her position. On the fourteenth of that month, after dating baseball's and America's heartthrob since 1952, Marilyn and Joe DiMaggio were married in San Francisco in a media event seen worldwide. During their honeymoon to Japan, Marilyn left her newlywed husband and traveled to Korea to entertain the troops in a USO show. She was so popular by this time that when she returned to Hollywood she was voted, "Most Popular Female Star," by *Photoplay* magazine. The studio finally reached an agreement with her and she was cast in *The Seven Year Itch* replete with a $100,000 bonus. This is the film that launched the iconic photo of Marilyn Monroe with her dress blowing up over a subway grate; the shot is what most people recognize as the quintessential Marilyn Monroe.

Still not content with Fox, Monroe moved to New York and formed her own production company—Marilyn Monroe Productions (MMP)—and filed suit against Fox, claiming they had violated her contract by not paying her bonus. This began a long legal battle that was instrumental in her marriage falling apart with Joltin' Joe. After her divorce in October of 1955, Marilyn met and married playwright Arthur Miller. Monroe and Fox settled their disagreement, and after Marilyn started working again, she began having to support Miller financially. It was about this time that Marilyn started to show signs of what today we would call bi-polar disorder. Norma Jean had always been afraid that she might succumb to the mental problems that ran in her family, and now those fears just might be realized. Marilyn enrolled in the prestigious Actors Studio in New York, which was run by Lee Strasberg. She became close friends with the Strasbergs and they would become the inheritors of Monroe's film and image rights after her death.

Back in Hollywood, Monroe was getting most of the parts she wanted, but she slowly began making a name for herself as somewhat of a troublemaker: she would constantly be late for film shoots—if she showed up at all—and decided to take an eighteen-month break to concentrate on her marriage. It was during this time that Marilyn began psychoanalysis at the urging of her friend, Strasberg. Marilyn became pregnant in 1957 but lost the baby due to endometriosis, a disease she'd had since puberty. This sent Marilyn into a deep depression, and to help combat it, she was prescribed Nembutal to help her sleep. Marilyn's mental state got so bad that she had to be committed for a time in a New York mental hospital. There is some speculation that Marilyn herself signed the papers admitting her to the psyche ward, and others say it was a close friend; whichever is true, Marilyn managed to sneak a message to DiMaggio who flew to New York and had her released.

Marilyn was still making huge sums of money for Fox, but the problems with her lateness to the set, difficulties in work ethics, and her drug use, which was made worse by the studios prescribing the Nembutal to her, as well as most of the actresses in Hollywood, were beginning to make the studio rethink having her under contract. It all started to come to a head after filming was complete on the film *Misfits*, a movie her now estranged husband, Arthur Miller, wrote specifically for her to star in. Monroe performed masterfully in the film and cemented herself as a serious actress, but her drug addiction was now fully engaged. Her husband began seeing other women, and when the film was finally completed, Marilyn went to Mexico and arranged for a speedy divorce. This film would be the last Marilyn Monroe would ever complete.

For a couple of years prior to 1962, there had been a persistent rumor that Monroe had been having an affair with President John F. Kennedy and his brother, Attorney General Robert Kennedy. The rumors of her dalliance with JFK are most likely not true, but Robert Kennedy may have had at least one romp with Marilyn, and is rumored to have been desperate for more. In a series of tapes Monroe recorded just before her death and given to her therapist Dr. Ralph Greenson, Marilyn said of the Kennedys: "As you can see, there is no room in my life for him [RFK]. I guess I don't have the courage to face up to it and hurt him. I want someone else to tell him it's over. I tried to get the president to do it, but I couldn't reach him." The communication between JFK and Marilyn was most likely only due to her affair with his brother, Bobby, and Monroe's desire to have him tell Robert it was over between them.

Marilyn was starring in the new film *Something's Got to Give* opposite Dean Martin. Nothing had changed, and the crew, director, and staff all had to endure Monroe's constant absence from the set, her late arrivals from her dressing room, and her stubbornness while filming. The next scene to be shot was of Marilyn swimming, supposedly naked, in a swimming pool while a nervous Dean Martin watched from a balcony. Marilyn had made arrangements with her photographer to be on set and ready to shoot her as she emerged from the pool actually naked. These photos would then be sold to *Playboy* as a way to boost her star appeal. The scene went off without a hitch, and when she finally came out of the pool sans clothes, she created quite the stir. The studio was not amused and said so to Monroe in no uncertain terms; they also informed her that she was not allowed to leave Hollywood until the film was completed, because they were already behind schedule and over budget due to her behavior. This last was because she had told them she was planning to attend JFK's birthday bash at Madison Square Garden. Even though she had been told not to leave, she went anyway, sang happy birthday to the president, and then immediately headed back to Hollywood. When she arrived back on set, she was informed that she was no longer part of the film or the studio and that they would be filing a breach of contract suit against her.

Marilyn Monroe bought this house to show everyone that she had "grown up;" it was through these gates that her dead body was brought out to a waiting ambulance.

Marilyn took her removal from the studio with her usual Scarlet O'Hara attitude, and to try to help repair her image after the studio went public, blaming her drug addiction and mental illness as the reasons for her being released, did several interviews with *Vogue*, *Life*, and *Cosmopolitan* magazines. The magazine pieces and photo shoots did help her reputation with the movie-going public, who still seemed to be enamored with their sex symbol, but it did nothing to help her get back into movies. Then, on August 5, 1962, Norma Jean Mortenson was found dead in her bedroom from an apparent suicide. Marilyn Monroe was dead and all the newspaper headlines read, ". . . Found Nude in Bed."

Marilyn Monroe was dead, but the story of her death was just beginning. Over the years, there has been much speculation on the actual cause of her death. There are those who say it was an obvious suicide, as she had tried to kill herself before; others say it was simply an accidental overdose caused by her addiction, and still others say she was murdered . . . by the Kennedys—and there may actually be some truth to this rumor.

We know from the records that Bobby Kennedy was in San Francisco the day that Marilyn died, and there are a few witnesses who have stated that they saw Kennedy at Monroe's home the day before she was found dead. These witnesses have all been vilified as glory seekers or liars or those just trying to jump on the fame bandwagon. These same detractors always point to the fact that there are no records of Kennedy flying to Los Angeles while in California that weekend, and it would have been too far of a drive and would have taken too long for him to have taken an incognito road trip and still make it back to the Bay in time for his meetings. In other words, there has always been a concerted effort to steer people away from this theory. Then, in 1992, Sam, Chuck, and Bettiana Giancana released the book *Double Cross: The Explosive*

Inside Story of the Mobster Who Controlled America (Warner Books March, 1992). In this book, they tell how the attorney general of the United States came to Marilyn's house on Saturday, August 4, with another gentleman, presumably a doctor, in an effort to get Marilyn to drop her threats about exposing personal details the family didn't want out in the public if Bobby didn't stop bothering her. At one point, Kennedy told the other man to "give her a shot to clam her down." This was an indication to the gangsters who were listening to proceed with the murder. After Kennedy and the other man left, the two killers waited until dark and then entered the home; there they tied up the barely struggling, sedated Monroe, donned rubber gloves, stripped her of her clothing and inserted a specially altered Nembutal suppository into her anus and waited for her to die. They then left the house as silently as they had entered.

The suppository that Giancana's men used on Marilyn Monroe was supposedly developed earlier for Sam Giancana to use in the assassination of the Castro brothers. The Kennedys had recruited Giancana for the job after the Bay of Pigs fiasco because of his ties to the Cuban drug trade. The Kennedys are well known to have had ties with the Giancana Crime Family of Chicago for many years, and it is believed that Giancana, being upset at the Kennedys for their hard stance against the Mafia, was responsible for the assassinations of both John and Robert Kennedy.

There are those who ask, "If Bobby was so in love with Marilyn, why would he have her killed?" It may be a case of family outweighing sex and the pursuit of power overcoming love. This need to clear her name and reputation of the charges of suicide and overdose, coupled with the quest for justice in her unsolved murder, may be the reason that Norma Jean is seen so frequently in so many places in and around Hollywood even to this day.

PARANORMAL ASSOCIATION

Perhaps the place where Marilyn Monroe is seen most often is at the famous Hollywood Roosevelt Hotel in downtown Hollywood. Marilyn seems to have formed an attachment to the place, maybe because it was here where her first moneymaking photo shoot took place and it was here that she stayed for a time while making that money—whatever reason, Marilyn likes it here. Her spirit is often seen in the bungalow where she lived while at the hotel; the guests who have witnessed her have stated that her ghost always appears pleasant and smiling. It's as if she is letting them know she doesn't mind sharing her suite with them.

Another area within the hotel—well, not an area per se but an object—is the full-length mirror that was once in the suite where Marilyn stayed. In 1985, just before the hotel was to reopen after a long renovation, one of the employees was busy cleaning the mirror—which at that time was in the general manager's office—and said she saw

Marilyn's grave has been kissed so often that it is now stained pink from lipstick.

the reflection of a "blonde girl" looking at her. When she turned around to ask the woman if she needed help, there was nobody there; when she went back to dusting the glass, she could again see the reflection of the woman who was still looking at her. Now, even though the employee never said the woman was Marilyn Monroe, most people believe that, since the mirror was where Marilyn would gaze at herself daily, she may have imprinted part of her spirit within the glass. The mirror has been moved a number of times, but at each location within the hotel, people have claimed to have seen the ghost of Marilyn reflected in the glass. (The mirror has since been sold and moved to the Roosevelt Hotel in New York City.)

Another place Monroe is said to haunt is her crypt in the tiny cemetery where she is buried. Over the years, so many people have come to pay their respects to Norma Jean that the face of her crypt has become stained pink from adoring fans kissing it while wearing deep red lipstick. This could account for the color of the mist that many have claimed to have witnessed emanating from in and around her final resting place. This rose-colored mist is said to appear out of nowhere, hover about for a time, and then fade back into the atmosphere from whence it came.

During her life Marilyn was embroiled in a scandal that had her sleeping with both President Kennedy and his brother, Bobby, at the same time. Both the Kennedys and Monroe were known to frequent the now-closed CalNeva Casino and Hotel on the border between California and Nevada at Lake Tahoe. Frank Sinatra owned the hotel in the early 1960s and, as a friend of Marilyn's, made sure that whenever she stayed at the lake she would have her own cabin; she was there often, and she always stayed in the same bungalow. At the time the resort closed its doors, there were still tunnels that led directly into both Sinatra's and Monroe's closets. Supposedly, these were left over from the Prohibition era, but during the tours that were given before the closure, it was pointed out that the tunnels also led directly to the room where Bobby Kennedy and his brother would always stay when at the hotel. Those who had rented the Monroe Cabin, as it was called, would report the feeling of being watched, the phantom aroma of perfume suddenly wafting through the air, and on rare occasions, guests have even said they have seen Marilyn sitting in the chair at the mirror. The tour guide who used to escort guests through the tunnels would always stop at a certain light hanging in the corridor near where the stairs leading to Monroe's secret closet entrance was located and tell how this was, "Marilyn's Light." He explained that it was a light that was permanently lit, with no switch to turn it off; he would go on to tell the guests how the light itself would turn off at odd times for no explanation and wouldn't come back on for days, even though maintenance would replace the bulb and check the wiring and all connections. He said that there were times when he would come down into the tunnels to find them dark and ask Marilyn nicely if she would turn the light on, and at that point, it would spring to life to light his way.

Rockhaven Sanitarium in the small town of Montrose, California, very near Hollywood, is another place where Marilyn Monroe's spirit has made an appearance, along with her mother. Gladys Baker, Norma Jean's mother, spent quite a few years here, and after Marilyn passed, a trust from her daughter's estate helped pay for her to remain at the women's rest home. While Marilyn was alive she would come here often to visit with her mother, and she once said that, "I can just be Norma when I am there with her." Gladys escaped from this sanitarium on a couple of occasions but was always found and brought back. Could it be that both mother and daughter are drawn to this place because here, they found the connection that they both had always wanted?

The place where Marilyn's spirit is seen the most is at her home, the place where she died. This home in Brentwood, California, was Marilyn's first and only house. She always took pride in the fact that she had earned the property with no outside help and felt it made her a "grown-up" in the eyes of her peers. Marilyn's spirit has reportedly been seen outside in the alley that serves as a street leading to her home's gate. There have been theories that Marilyn was still alive when she was removed from the house and died as she was being placed into the ambulance to be taken to the hospital. Once she passed, however, her friend and brother-in-law of the president, Peter Lawford, ordered her body to be placed back in her bed so incriminating evidence of foul play could be removed and for the enema to have more time to dissolve within her body. I find this theory to be highly suspect as that would have to mean that even the police, coroner, and ambulance personnel would had to have been involved in the cover up. That does not mean, however, that her ghost would be restricted to the property. Ms. Monroe could be wandering outside her gates as a way to draw attention to herself in the hopes that her murder may one day be discovered. Marilyn has also been seen by the current homeowners sitting by the pool and wandering the hallways. One report stated that while lying in bed in the room where Marilyn passed away, one of the residents felt someone get into bed with them; when they looked, no one was there. These stories are unsubstantiated regarding her old home and, therefore, taken with a grain of salt as to their validity.

As a side note, Robert Kennedy, the man most likely to have ordered her killed, if indeed she was murdered, was shot and killed a short distance away from Hollywood at The Ambassador Hotel on June 5, 1968, just after winning the California Democratic primary. He was gunned down and hit several times by Sirhan Sirhan. Kennedy died the following day. The hotel has since closed and been demolished to make way for a high school; however, before it was shut down there were many reports of Bobby's spirit being seen in the kitchen passageway where he was shot, as well as in the ballroom where he gave his victory speech that night. Once the school itself was built—it was designed to look just like the old Ambassador Hotel—children would report to their teachers and school staff that they were, "seeing a man who wasn't there." The school is still there but no reports of ghostly activity persist, either because the spirit has left or no one is allowed to talk about it.

The Robert F. Kennedy Community Schools now stand where the Ambassador Hotel and Coconut Grove nightclub once stood. A spirit believed to be that of Kennedy still haunts the school to this day.

The conspiracy theories surrounding Marilyn Monroe's death started almost from the day she died. Some are farfetched, such as the one stating that her death was a part of a communist conspiracy and another that her housekeeper and companion, Eunice Murray, had administered the fatal enema. There is even one that says missing mobster Jimmy Hoffa personally did the deed seeking revenge on Bobby Kennedy. My personal favorite, however, is the theory that either the CIA or FBI killed Marilyn to get the Kennedys attention and to use the murder as a "point of pressure against the Kennedys."

Conspiracy theories aside, the life of Norma Jean Baker was one of sorrow and loss, a life of searching for something she had lost but wasn't sure exactly what that was, confusion, mental illness, and a profound feeling of being used by those around her but mostly the men she so desperately wanted to have love her. I could not separate the girl, Norma Jean, from the woman, Marilyn Monroe, as I was doing my research and found myself drawn to the innate innocence that never really left this child sex symbol. All I can say is, "Yes, Norma Jean, I laid my eyes on you and I see you!"

CHAPTER 8

RAMON NOVARRO

Ramon Novarro's Walk of Fame star at 6350 Hollywood Boulevard.

When asked to think of a Latin lover from filmdom, most people will automatically picture Rudolph Valentino in their minds. Valentino was indeed who most women of that era dreamt about, and even today his image is used as the quintessential archetype. There is, however, another male sex symbol from that period who women adored, gave Valentino competition, and was, in fact, Valentino's protégé. He was also brutally murdered by two young men in his own home, and to this day remains at the site so no one will forget.

Born Jose Ramon Samaniego in Durango, Mexico, in 1899, to a wealthy family, his dentist father became concerned that the Mexican revolution would endanger his family and decided that a move to the United States would be the safest course of action. As Jose grew up, he became enamored with films and decided that was what he wanted to do with his life. He was working in 1917 as a singing waiter and auditioning for roles but was only cast in bit parts. Even though his appearances were small, he was making connections within the industry. Two of these who became friends, director Rex Ingram and his wife, Alice Terry, knew that he could have a great career in the movies and began promoting him as a rival to Rudolph Valentino. They also urged him to change his name to something easier to pronounce. Jose was a close friend with Gabriel Navarro, the grandfather of rocker Dave Navarro, founder of the group Jane's Addiction. Jose decided to use his friend's last name as his stage name and his own middle name, Ramon, but a typing error occurred, forever changing his name to Novarro.

All of the campaigning for Novarro paid off as he was slowly offered bigger roles; in 1923, he appeared in the movie *Scaramouch,* and the film became a major success. When he was given the title role in the movie *Ben-Hur: A Tale of the Christ*, his revealing costumes and charisma made him a household name. All of a sudden, he began living up to the hype of being Valentino's rival in Hollywood. The truth was anything but that, as rumors of Valentino taking Novarro under his wing to teach him the ins and outs of being a Hollywood sex symbol spread.

Ramon Novarro had been brought up in a strict Catholic household; for most of his life Ramon knew there was something different about him, and when he finally realized that he was gay, he made peace with his sexuality but could never make peace with his religion and their views on homosexual behavior. Once Novarro hit it big in Hollywood, he was very discreet about his proclivities and his handlers at MGM made sure it stayed that way. When Novarro got himself into trouble at a club, Louis B. Mayer himself covered up the affair and went so far as to push Novarro into a "lavender marriage," as it was called in those days, which Novarro emphatically refused to even consider. When Rudolph Valentino died in 1926, Novarro became his replacement in front of the camera for the thousands of women who mourned their sex idol, but Ramon, unbeknownst to the masses, mourned right along with them, for he had lost someone he loved.

Novarro found solace in the arms of his publicist and well-known journalist of the time, Herbert Howe. He continued to perform and make money for MGM and was one of only a handful of actors to be able to make the transition from silent pictures to "talkies" without much trouble. As the 1920s faded into the new decade, Novarro began drinking heavily and had bouts of depression, which made him drink even more. His battle within himself over his homosexuality seemed to lessen only when he was drunk. In 1935, Novarro's contract with MGM had expired, and the studio failed to renew his contract. He began making his rounds to the different studios and was finally signed by Republic Pictures, where he made a couple of films but could not seem to revive his glory days—it seemed as if his star power had faded. Over the next few years, Novarro struggled to find work: He took roles wherever he could find them, including film noir pieces and even a Mexican-made drama film. In the 1950s, he managed to garner more bit parts in a few westerns, and as television came on the scene, he was hired for parts in shows such as *Walt Disney Presents, Dr. Kildare, Combat, Bonanza* and *The Wild Wild West*.

Novarro had always been a good businessman and had invested his money wisely in real estate and other ventures. In 1928, Novarro hired Lloyd Wright to design what would become known as the Novarro-Samuel House in the Hollywood Hills. The home was a gift for his personal secretary, Louis Samuel; Novarro would own the home, but Samuel could live there for as long as he wanted. The two eventually had a falling out and Novarro would move in, but when his money began to dry up for lack of work, Novarro finally sold the home and moved into a more modest dwelling in Laurel Canyon. The amount of money he made from the sale along with the money still in reserve allowed Novarro to be comfortable for the rest of his life.

Ramon Novarro was a lonely man; he wanted and needed companionship—not necessarily sex, although that was hoped for, but the simple touch and pleasure of the company of other men. Always discreet, Novarro didn't like the idea of going to bars or clubs to look for men; he felt that this was a turkey shoot, a game of chance where you might not find a respectable, safe gentleman to spend the evening with, and being in a public place raised the risk of his exposure to the press. Novarro found a service very near his home that specialized in male escorts and would call them for his needs whenever he felt lonely; he gained the reputation among the men of the service as a kindly old gentleman who paid very well, whether he had sex with you or not. Most of the escorts were anxious to be called to Novarro's home.

Ramon Novarro's original home has been replaced, but the home is said to be haunted by the silent film star even today.

On October 30, 1968, Novarro received a call from Paul Ferguson saying that Masseurs, the escort service Ramon used, had given him his number and was told to call about providing service for the evening. In actuality Ferguson had gotten Novarro's phone number from a friend who knew Novarro was always interested in meeting nice young men and thought that Novarro might be able to help Paul's brother, Tommy, who had just arrived in Los Angeles from Chicago. Both Paul and Tommy Ferguson had worked as "hustlers" to make ends meet for some time and knew about Ramon Novarro from a television interview they had recently seen. Paul told Ramon about his brother and asked if he could bring him along on the "date" the following day and Ramon eagerly agreed.

The following day Paul and Tommy Ferguson hitchhiked from their home to West Hollywood to the apartment of one of Paul's friends who gave them a ride the rest of the way to Novarro's house. They arrived around 4:30, knocked on the door, and were met by Novarro, dressed in a red and blue silk robe; he invited them inside. Ramon immediately offered them chairs and asked if they would like anything to drink; Paul had vodka while Tommy drank tequila chased with beer. The three settled in to get to know each other and seemed to be getting along very well. Novarro, trying to compliment Paul in an obvious play of seduction, told him that with his features he could be a big star in Hollywood—he could be another Clint Eastwood. He even went so far as to call a press agent friend of his to set up a meeting between the two. He read Paul's palm and told him that he was going to have a long life, and Paul even went to the piano and banged on the keys in a childish rendition of "Chopsticks." While Ramon was busy seducing Paul, Tommy had been looking around the living room, glancing behind pictures and generally snooping about. In Ramon Novarro's mind, the evening with these two beautiful young men was just what he'd needed.

After a dinner of chicken gizzards, Tommy settled back into the living room, and Ramon and Paul went into the master bedroom. Here is where the story has taken a few different directions: one is from the viewpoint of the murderers, one from the press, and one pieced together by the detectives and coroners from the Los Angeles Police Department. I will try to give as accurate an account as possible, but only those actually present will ever know the truth of what happened that night. It would seem that while Paul was in the bedroom distracting Novarro, Tommy was busy searching the rest of the house for $5,000 they believed Novarro had hidden there. Tommy was unable to find it and then somehow let his brother know that he had come up empty. At this point, Paul began to demand that Ramon tell them where the money was hidden, but the kindly old man kept telling them he had no idea what they were talking about. Paul began hitting Novarro and telling him he would stop if he would just give them the cash.

Meanwhile, Tommy was back in the living room on the telephone talking to his girlfriend of only a few months, who lived in Chicago; he was busy telling her that they were at a movie star's house and was working on trying to get enough money for her to fly to California so they could get married. Tom told her that his brother, Paul, knew that there was $5,000 hidden in the house somewhere and that he was upstairs now trying to find out where Ramon had put it. Tom's girlfriend told police that while she was on the phone she could hear yelling and the sounds of someone screaming in pain. That's when Tom told her, "I have to go before my brother really hurts Ramon, and I want to find out what's going on." Tom then hung up the phone.

When Tom got back to Novarro's bedroom, he found that the old man had been severely beaten; his face was puffy and looked blue from all of the bruising, the back of his head was bleeding, and he was trying to plead with them through lips so swollen little sound could escape between them. Tom took the naked and bleeding Novarro into the bathroom to clean him up and then put him back on the bed; as the brothers looked down at the old man, Ramon took one more shuddering breath as he looked up at his two tormentors, closed his eyes, and never opened them again. Paul and Tom Ferguson took $20 they found in Novarro's robe and then fled the house.

Novarro's personal secretary, Edward Weber, arrived for work at 8:30 as he did every morning and let himself in through the kitchen door; it was October 31, Halloween, and he was about to walk into a house of horrors. Ed walked into the living room and saw that the room was in shambles: furniture was overturned and all of the pictures were off the walls and strewn over the floor, Weber started calling for Novarro; when he received no answer, he began searching the house, entering the master bedroom and looking around; but couldn't find his boss. He went to the window and drew the curtains open to let the sunlight in, stood there for a moment to let his eyes adjust to the light, and then turned to leave—that's when he saw Ramon Novarro lying nude on the king size bed, his body so badly beaten that he was almost unrecognizable. Weber rushed to the phone and called the police; he then phoned Novarro's brother and Ramon's priest. Ater that he called Leonard Shannon, Novarro's friend and publicist, and told him, "Len, you better come right over. This is it; Ramon's been murdered."

When the police arrived, who were followed by a mob of journalists, what they found was something out of a horror film. The reporters were traipsing all over the property looking for the best shot for their newspapers or television newscasts and inadvertently helped the investigation by finding a pile of bloody clothes hidden in ivy on the other side of a tall fence in the lot next door. These were Paul's and were put there by Tom while his brother donned some of Novarro's clothes he'd found in the closet. The preliminary coroner's report stated that: "Blood noted on the floor in bedroom, on ceiling and tooth noted lying on floor at foot of bed. Decedent's hands were tied behind his back with brown electric cord, (a white condom was found in decedent's right hand) and electric cord extended down and was tied around decedent's ankles. Lacerations and ecchymosis were noted on face and head." When the final autopsy report was released, it said that Novarro's blood alcohol level was .23, well above today's legal limit. He had a fractured nose with bruising on his head, chest, and neck, left arm, knee, and penis. The cause of death was determined to be, "suffocation by choking on his own blood caused by multiple traumatic injuries of the face, neck, nose, and mouth."

The discovery of the bloody clothes, along with the records that showed that Novarro's phone had been used to call Chicago during the time that the coroner placed as the time of death, led investigators to the Chicago home of Brenda Lee Metcalf, Tom's girlfriend. Faced with the interrogation by detectives, Metcalf told them everything that Tom had said during the phone call, including her hearing the screams and moans of Novarro as Paul had been torturing him. After the investigators arrived back in California, it didn't take them long to apprehend and arrest the Ferguson brothers. The trial of Paul and Tom Ferguson began on July 28, 1969, and started out as one of the biggest news stories of the year; it was all but forgotten twelve days later when, on August 9, the bodies of Sharon Tate and her house guests were found butchered in her home on Cielo Drive. Both Paul and Tom were found guilty and sentenced to life to be served in San Quentin Prison.

PARANORMAL ASSOCIATION

Ramon Novarro now sleeps all but forgotten in a lonely
East Los Angeles cemetery.

Ramon Novarro led a lonely life; he was a homosexual and his fear of being found out, which at the time could have ruined his career, along with his being torn between his feelings for men and his strict Catholic upbringing would, in the end, never allow him to find true happiness. The reason that Paul Ferguson thought that Novarro had $5,000 stashed in his home was due to the young man misunderstanding what Novarro had said in response to a question he had seen the old man answer on a television talk show. Novarro was asked about a renovation he had just completed inside his home and said, "I have $5,000 in my living room." No one ever accused the Fergusons of being intelligent. This along with his brutal torture and murder by two young men he thought could be friends and lovers could explain why Ramon has not yet passed on from this realm of existence.

Novarro's house in Laurel Canyon has been demolished and a new home rebuilt since the murder occurred, but over the years, quite a few owners of the property have claimed to have seen Ramon within the house. There was even one buyer who bought the house because Ramon haunted it. Novarro was often seen in the bedroom by those living there: they would claim to watch as his spirit casually walked between the bed and the bathroom and then disappear once he reached the shower. This may be a residual haunt; it is well known that strong emotions just before death can leave an imprint in the area that will be repeated over and over like a video that keeps playing on a loop. Other visitors to the home have said that they have felt what they called, "an uneasy" feeling within the home. This phenomenon occurs mainly in the living room and dining room, an area where Novarro and the Ferguson brothers had spent time getting to know each other. Could this be a residual feeling that Novarro may have felt but ignored while in the presence of Paul and Tom? A TV host and her crew felt this same feeling of unease in the 1980s when Connie Chung filmed at the house for a segment about Ramon Novarro. At the time, several members of the film crew refused to enter the house; they said that as they began going into the home, an eerie feeling hit them and affected them so badly that they could not bring themselves to go past the threshold of the front door.

Once the house where Novarro had been murdered was demolished, the owners had been sure that the hauntings would go away. This was not to be the case. As many paranormal enthusiasts know, the simple destruction of a location usually has no effect on the spirits that may be present. After the new house was built, all of the occurrences started back up and all of the reports remained the same as before. Not only did the hauntings continue but, as often happens during renovations with construction or complete change of building parameters, the hauntings may have actually increased. There have now been reports from neighbors and passersby of hearing screams and moans of pain, presumably from Novarro's spirit reliving his last horrific hours of life.

Today, we live in a world that is more tolerant than the one Ramon Novarro endured. Our perceptions of gays, lesbians, and transgender people have evolved, one hopes, into a more open and less judgmental point of view. We all must regrettably understand that prejudice still exists, but we hope that the bigotry is not shown in violent outbursts. To live as Novarro did should never happen; love should be blind, and as a society it should be none of our business who one loves. The act of love itself should be enough in a world where it is sorely lacking. Let us hope that Ramon sees this evolution and can finally be at peace.

The murders of Sharon Tate and her unborn child sent shock
waves across America and the world.

The name Charles Manson alone conjures up images of death and hate. Even for those too young to remember the brutal slayings he and his followers committed, the name is still known. Today, sadly, Manson has more followers then he did in those dark days of 1969 when his deranged mind tried to start a race war by killing innocent people and blaming the murders on the Black Panthers. Sadder still, is that some of his victims may not have gone on to their rest but remain to relive their tragic ends.

Manson was born in Cincinnati, Ohio, in 1934, to a sixteen-year-old single mother, who was also an alcoholic, by the name of Kathleen Maddox. According to Manson, his mother once sold him to a childless waitress for a pitcher of beer, and his uncle had to retrieve him days later. When Charles was born his birth certificate simply said, "No name Maddox." It took Kathleen quite awhile, but finally she settled on Charles for her son's name and had the document changed. While Charles was still very young, Kathleen married a man by the name of William Manson; the marriage didn't last long, but Charles decided to take William's last name as his own.

When Charles was just five years old, his mother was convicted of robbery and sentenced to five years in jail. While she was incarcerated, young Charlie stayed with his aunt and uncle in West Virginia until his mother came and got him after she was paroled in 1942. For the next five years, Kathleen and Charlie moved from one seedy hotel room to another. She would drink, and Charlie would look after her when she came home drunk.

At the age of thirteen, Manson's mother tried to have him placed into foster care, but as there were no homes available at that time, the courts intervened and he was sent to Gibault School for Boys in Indiana. After only ten months at the school, Charles ran away and went home to be with his mother, but she rejected him and sent him away. Soon Charlie was living on the streets. To get enough money to rent rooms to stay in, he began robbing grocery stores and small shops but was eventually caught and sent to a boy's detention center; he escaped the following day. He was recaptured and sent to Boy's Town, but again, after only a short stay, he once more escaped. Now a teenager, Manson was again caught and sent to the Indiana Boys School. He once more escaped but this time with the help of two other boys.

The three boys survived by committing armed robbery and car theft as they worked their way west. While trying to steal a car in Utah, the boys were caught, and because Manson was now seventeen and the crime was a federal offense, he was deemed "aggressively anti-social" and was sent to prison. Manson was anything but a model citizen while in prison; he had a string of violent encounters, and there is even a story that he sodomized another boy with the help of other inmates. He was finally paroled in 1954 and moved back in with his mother for a brief time.

The following year, Charles met a young woman by the name of Rosalie Jean Willis. Rosalie was a hospital waitress, and Manson was so taken by her that he married her that same year. He was twenty-one and she was only seventeen. Manson supported them by taking small, odd jobs and by stealing cars. In 1956, Manson decided to head to California with his now-pregnant wife. He stole a car to drive them to the West Coast, with Rosalie oblivious to the fact that Charlie was back to his old ways of crime. Manson said that in the short time they were married he had found, "marital bliss," but it was not to last long.

Upon arrival in California, Manson again began committing robberies and stealing cars, and it wasn't long before he was again arrested. This time Manson wasn't a juvenile, and he was sentenced to three years at Terminal Island Federal Penitentiary in San Pedro, California, one of the most violent prisons in the state. Rosalie gave birth to a son shortly after Manson was incarcerated, Charles Milles Manson Jr. At first Rosalie would come visit Charlie in jail, but the visits became further apart and eventually stopped altogether. Manson found out from his mother that Rosalie was living with another man; she divorced him soon after, the same year Charlie was paroled from prison.

Now that Manson was free again, he decided to try his hand at prostitution; Charlie began pimping a sixteen-year-old girl, but the money wasn't what he expected, and he looked for a way to supplement his income. He met another young girl and convinced her to help him financially by taking money from her wealthy parents. He was arrested again in 1959, this time for attempting to cash a stolen Treasury check. Manson was sentenced to ten years in prison, but a woman by the name of Leona "Candy" Stevens, who was known by the court due to her own past arrest record for prostitution, made an emotional plea on his behalf. Stevens tearfully told the court that if Manson were released, they would be married and both their lives would be turned from crime. The judge granted her appeal and Charlie had his ten-year sentence suspended and was given probation instead.

Manson and Stevens were soon married, and they had a child, another son for Charlie, by the name of Charles Luther Manson. The two moved to New Mexico where "Candy" again worked as a prostitute along with another girl they had met along the way. Manson was again under the watchful eye of law enforcement and was brought in and questioned for violation of the Mann Act (also known as the White Slave Traffic Act). He was released, but the investigation continued, so Charlie and Leona moved to Laredo, Texas. A bench warrant was issued under the Mann Act, and Manson was picked up in Texas in June of 1960. He was sent back to California for violation of his probation and ordered to serve out his ten-year sentence. Leona finally divorced Charlie in 1963.

After serving five years at McNeil Federal Penitentiary in Washington State, Manson was again sent to Terminal Island in preparation for an early release. While in prison, Manson had taken a study course written by Dale Carnegie. In his book *How to Win Friends and Influence People*, published in 1936, Carnegie shares his salesmanship techniques for manipulating others into doing what you want them to do. This, along with the teachings he'd learned from his time as a follower of the Church of Scientology, would allow Manson to brainwash members of the growing hippie movement once he was released from prison.

March 21, 1967, was Charles Manson's release date; he was thirty-two years old and had spent most of his life behind bars. As the day approached, Manson begged the prison officials not to let him out; he told them that, "prison is my home" and made a formal request to stay. It was denied. He then asked to be allowed to travel to the San Francisco Bay area of California, which was the hub of the new Hippie movement. He told officials that the "Peace and Freedom" movement would be good for him. This request was granted.

Upon his release from Terminal Island, Manson moved to Berkeley, California, where he survived mostly by panhandling. He soon met a twenty-three-year old by the name of Mary Brunner, who was working at the Berkeley University library, and moved in with her. Over time, he convinced Brunner to overlook the other women he brought to their apartment, and they eventually had eighteen women living with them. Manson soon began preaching a strange philosophical mix of Satanism, Christianity, and Scientology, along with the "Summer of Love" way of life to a group of followers in San Francisco's Haight-Ashbury. Manson was considered some kind of guru, and they began calling themselves Manson's family; most of these followers were female. They found an old school bus and fixed it up "Hippie" style with colored pillows, drapes, and rugs, and then headed out to Washington State. Manson was again in violation of parole.

This cave behind the movie town of Spahn Ranch is
where *LIFE* magazine took the photograph of the Manson "family"
and forever dubbed this the "Manson Family Cave."
(*Photo Courtesy of Gerald S. Reynolds*)

The Manson family roamed the Southwest going to Washington, Nevada, Arizona, New Mexico, and back to Los Angeles—wherever Manson told them to go, they went. He had gained complete control over his followers. They would take turns driving; Manson would send them out to scrounge or steal food and the supplies they needed, and Charlie would play the guitar, sing, and preach his message, the family hanging on his every word. They arrived back in California in late 1967 and set up housekeeping in an abandoned house in Topanga Canyon.

Mary Brunner was pregnant by the time they drove back to Los Angeles, and she gave birth to Charlie's third son, Valentine Michael Manson, or Pooh Bear, as he was called. Manson now fancied himself as a singer/songwriter and began searching for ways to break into the recording industry. He had a passing relationship with a Hollywood actor who introduced him to a Universal Studio's producer, but that went nowhere. Luck finally struck for Manson in late 1968, when Beach Boy's drummer Dennis Wilson, picked up two of his followers, Ella Jo Bailey and Patricia Krenwinkel, while they were hitchhiking. Wilson drove the two women to his Pacific Palisades home and allowed them to spend the night; they left the next morning and headed back to the ranch where they had taken up residence. Later that day, when the drummer returned home from a recording session, he found Charlie waiting for him in his driveway.

Manson and a few of his girls took to crashing at Wilson's house, He was introduced to some of the music industry's biggest people, including Neil Young; John Phillips of the Mamas and the Papas; and Terry Melcher, the producer for the Byrds. Brian Wilson, Dennis' brother; and leader of the Beach Boys even gave Charlie time in his recording studio. Manson's demanding attitude and intolerance for the orders of the studio personnel doomed his music career; the Beach Boys did release two songs Manson wrote for the group: "Never Learn Not To Love," was released on their album *20/20*, and "Cease To Resist," was released on the B-side of their 45 "Bluebirds Over The Mountain." The original title Manson created was "Cease To Exist," and its lyrics and music gives us just a glint into Manson's fragile sanity.

At first, Dennis Wilson tolerated Manson and his followers because Manson always had a ready supply of drugs, and the girls acted as servants for both of the men, which included as many sexual favors as Dennis wanted. Over time, however, Wilson realized that Manson's philosophies were becoming dangerous, and that if he allowed them to stay, Wilson could get caught up in something he might regret. There is some speculation that he contracted a venereal disease from Manson's women, and that hastened their removal. It was Dennis Wilson's manager who finally kicked the family out of Wilson's house.

After Charlie and his followers were removed from Wilson's Sunset Boulevard home, they found refuge in Chatsworth, California, at the Spahn Movie Ranch. This ranch was originally owned by silent film actor William S. Hart; the "wild west town" was used in numerous westerns and TV shows, including *The Lone Ranger, Zorro, Bonanza,* and the 1946 hit movie *Duel In The Sun.* Disheartened by the state of Hollywood, Hart sold the ranch to George Spahn in 1948. By the time Manson and his cult moved to the ranch in 1968, Spahn was eighty years old. In need of extra help around the property, Spahn allowed the family to live rent-free in exchange for work. They would do daily chores, which included feeding the horses at the stables, renting horses to tourists—which was the ranch's main source of income—and picking up droppings, as well as performing maintenance on the buildings. To help solidify his hold on Spahn, Manson ordered his girls to occasionally have sex with the old man. It was Spahn who gave Lynette Fromme her nickname "Squeaky" due to the noise she made whenever he touched her leg.

Manson had still not given up on his dream of becoming a famous recording artist, and while the family was working around the ranch, Charlie would be wandering Hollywood looking for contacts to make his dream a reality. Terry Melcher, son of Doris Day, and Candice Bergen's lover, was one of those Manson sought help from.

Melcher was at one time going to help Manson get a recording contract, but because of the difficulties everyone had with Manson, Melcher backed out—no matter how many times Charlie approached him, Melcher told him no. At the time, Terri Melcher, along with Candice Bergen lived at 10050 Cielo Drive.

The gates and address have been changed,
but behind this portal, one of the most gruesome killings
of the twentieth century took place.

Manson didn't handle rejection well, and with both Wilson and now Melcher turning on him, Charlie began his slide into complete madness. Manson began preaching about the race war that was coming and that there was no way to stop it; the only thing that could be done was to control it. He told his followers that the "Blackies" were destined to win this war over the "Whities," but that they would be unable to govern afterwards. Manson began doing large amounts of LSD and exerted complete control over his family. He told them that the only way to survive was to dig a "bottomless pit" to hide in until the war was over and then emerge to take control, to be the power behind the Black governments of the world. Charles "Tex" Watson became one of Manson's most devout followers and his right-hand man during this time.

In preparation for this war, the family headed out to Death Valley. One of the new girls who joined the family had relatives at the Myers Ranch just east of the Panamint Mountains. The family stayed at this ranch briefly until they met the owner of the Barker Ranch, who let them stay there as long as they wanted for helping with the upkeep of the place. The Barker Ranch was perfect for Charlie's needs: it was extremely remote, had plenty of places to construct his hideaway from the race wars, and would be well out of the eyesight of law enforcement.

The family left the desert in January 1969 and headed back to Los Angeles; this time, however, they decided to rent a house close to the Spahn Ranch. The house was a bright canary yellow color, and Charlie dubbed it the "Yellow Submarine" after one of the Beatles's songs that Charlie liked—Manson had become obsessed with the Beatles. After hearing the newly released *White Album*, Manson became convinced that the band had hidden messages in the songs directed at him and his place in the coming race wars. He believed that the song "Helter Skelter" foretold the coming war and that they, the Beatles, were behind Manson. Charlie told his followers that when the time came, the Fab Four would be with them.

Within a few weeks of renting the house, Manson turned it into a drug pad, adult movie studio, and place where car thieves could come and part out their stolen rides. Even though many of Manson's Hollywood buddies had turned their backs on him, they now found themselves drawn back because of his new party pad, and even Dennis Wilson and Terry Melcher found themselves at the Yellow Submarine having sex with Manson's girls and partaking of Manson's drugs. Even after Manson's arrest, Melcher would try to say that he was never there; after showing investigators a picture of his lover, Candice Bergen, he was quoted as saying, "When I have beauties like these to get in bed with, why would I want to screw any of Manson's clap-ridden, unwashed dogs?"

The single-story ranch house has been replaced, but the view remains as the reason the property was so coveted.

By now, the crowd was growing, and the house was beginning to draw the attention of the neighbors. Manson knew it was just a matter of time before the police were called. Charlie went back to speak with George Spahn, and even though Spahn and Manson were on good terms, Manson could tell that some of the ranch hands were not happy to see him again. One of these was Donald "Shorty" Shea. Manson asked Spahn if the family could come back to live at the ranch; Spahn was happy to oblige but told Manson that someone was already living in the other house but that the old movie town was available. Manson agreed and told Spahn, "Don't worry George, the girls will take good care of you." The smile and wink from Spahn told Charlie that the ranch was again his.

Now back at the ranch, work began in earnest on the preparations for the coming war. The family would steal Volkswagen Beetles and strip them down, turning them into dune buggies. These were to be used in the desert in and around their "bottomless pit" city where they would wait to reemerge. Manson would write songs daily by a tree on the ranch that were to tell the tale of the coming race war and would become the family's world-changing album. Manson had told them that Melcher was coming to hear them sing the songs, and that once he did, their message would go out to the world. In preparation for his arrival, the whole town was cleaned, meals were cooked, and the girls were made ready to please him. Terry Melcher never came.

On March 23, 1969, Manson went to Melcher's house at 10050 Cielo Drrive to speak with him about his absence at the ranch. Melcher had moved out of this house in February; Roman Polanski and his wife, Sharon Tate, now rented the home. As Manson approached the house, Shahrokh Hatami, a personal friend of Sharon Tate's and also her photographer, met him. Hatami had seen Manson approach and had gone out onto the porch to see what he wanted. Manson told him that he was looking for Melcher, but Hatami didn't recognize the name and so told Manson, "This is the Polanski residence. Maybe you should try the back alley." About this time, Tate came to the door, asked Hatami who was calling and looked directly at Manson. Charlie started to walk down to the guesthouse, but then turned around and left. Manson returned later and went to the guesthouse where he spoke with Rudi Altobelli, the owner of the property, asking for Melcher. Vincent Bugliosi, who was the prosecutor in the murder trials later, said that Manson already knew that Terry Melcher had moved out, so why Manson would have returned to the home looking for him is a mystery. Altobelli had met Charlie the previous year at Dennis Wilson's home during a party and figured Manson remembered him. He told Manson that Melcher had moved to Malibu and then lied about not knowing the location or the address. Altobelli then told Manson that he was getting ready to leave town for a year and to please stop bothering his tenants. The next day, Rudi Altobelli flew to Rome with Sharon Tate who asked him if "that creepy-looking guy" had spoken to him. Rudi pointedly avoided the question.

Manson was now sure that the race war was close at hand and sent Tex Watson out on a mission to gather money that the family would use when they came out of hiding after it was all over. Watson knew a black drug dealer by the name of Bernard "Lotsapoppa" Crowe and began defrauding him; when Crowe found out about the scam, he publicly threatened to wipe out Manson and everyone at Spahn Ranch along with him. Manson then went to Crowe's Hollywood apartment and shot him; although Crowe survived the assault, Manson believed that he had killed the man. Manson was under the mistaken belief that Crowe was a member of the Black Panthers and that they would seek revenge on the family for his murder. A news report following the shooting also mistakenly stated that Crowe was killed and had been a member of the Panthers. Believing that an attack was eminent, Manson had his followers gathered as many weapons as they could find and turned Spahn Ranch into an armed camp. They instituted night patrols and placed armed guards around the perimeters. Tex Watson later said, "If we'd needed any more proof that Helter Skelter was coming down very soon, this was it. Blackie was trying to get to the chosen ones."

Manson had found out that an acquaintance of his by the name of Gary Hinman had just come into some money from an inheritance, and as Manson already mistakenly believed that Hinman owned the house he was living in and had money in stocks and bonds, he sent family members Bobby Beausoleil, Susan Atkins, and Mary Brunner to Hinman's house to convince him to join the family. This would mean that Hinman would have to turn over all his assets to Manson. When the three cultists arrived at the house, Hinman was polite but emphatically said no and asked them to leave. In an effort to convince Hinman to change his mind, Beausoleil tied Hinman to a chair and began to hit him. Hinman, a pacifist Buddhist, just kept asking them to leave, but Beausoleil ignored him.

The next day, Manson and follower Bruce Davis showed up at Hinman's; when Gary still refused to give Manson what he wanted, Manson went into a rage, picked up a sword and struck Hinman in the side of his head, deeply slicing his ear. Hinman looked up at Charlie and just kept asking, "Why are you doing this? Please, just leave." Manson then spoke briefly to Beausoleil, grabbed Hinman's car keys, and left with Davis in tow. After Manson and Davis left, Susan Atkins and Mary Brunner stitched up Hinman's ear with a sewing needle and dental floss while Beausoleil continued the beatings. The next day, sure that Hinman was not going to cooperate, Bobby Beausoleil picked up a knife and drove the blade twice into Gary Hinman's chest. The three took turns holding a pillow over his face until they were sure he was dead. Before they left, Beausoleil and the girls, using Hinman's blood wrote, "political piggy" on the wall with a Black Panther paw print next to it in an attempt to place the blame on the Panthers. Bobby Beausoleil was arrested on August 6 while sleeping in Hinman's car. Gary Allen Hinman died July 27, 1969.

Manson now believed that the blacks were incapable of starting the war on their own and would need help from him and his followers. On the night of August 8, Manson gathered his family at Spahn Ranch and told them, "Now is the time for Helter Skelter." He then directed Tex Watson to take Linda Kasabian, Patricia Krenwinkel, and Susan Atkins, "to that house were Melcher used to live and destroy everyone in it as gruesome as you can." He then told the women to do whatever Watson told them to do.

That evening Sharon Tate had asked her friend and former lover Jay Sebring if he could keep her company because her husband, movie director Roman Polanski, was away in Europe, and she was nervous because she was eight months pregnant. After a nice dinner out at Sharon's favorite Mexican restaurant, El Coyote, with Sebring, coffee heiress Abigail Folger, and her lover, Wojciech Frykowski, the four headed back to Tate's house at 10050 Cielo Drive in the Benedict Canyon area of Beverly Hills.

This is the same telephone pole Charles "Tex" Watson used to gain entry to the property the night of the murders.

Once there, they settled in for a long, relaxing evening with each other. What they didn't know was that while they were busy enjoying each other's company, Tex Watson was climbing the telephone pole outside the gates of the estate and cutting the telephone lines. After Watson came down, the four family members climbed the embankment next to the gate and dropped onto the grounds of the property. Almost immediately, headlights coming up the drive from the guesthouse illuminated them. Watson ordered the women to hide in the bushes while he stepped out and stopped the car. The driver, eighteen-year-old Steven Parent hit the brakes while Watson leveled a .22 pistol at him (the same gun used to shoot Crowe) and approached the car. The boy was terrified and pleaded with Watson not to hurt him. Watson, unmoved, lunged at the boy with the knife he had in his other hand, but Parent raised his arm which deflected the blade, cutting his palm and severing his watch. Watson then leveled the gun at Parent and shot the boy four times in the chest and stomach. Parent had been visiting the property's caretaker, nineteen-year-old William Garretson, who lived alone in the guesthouse, and now had become the first victim of the evening for the Manson cult.

After moving the car into hiding, Watson and the three women ran across the front lawn and searched for an open window. Watson had to cut a screen, but they had found their way into the home. Watson sent Kasabian back to Parent's car to keep watch with orders to alert them if there was anyone coming, and then he entered the house through the open window, carefully made his way to the front door, and opened it for Atkins and Krenwinkel. By now, Tate and Sebring were alone in Tate's bedroom talking quietly, Folger was in her room reading, and Frykowski had fallen asleep on the couch. As they stole through the house, Watson was giving orders to Susan Atkins, which woke Frykowski. Not realizing what was happening, Frykowski mumbled, "What time is it?" Tex Watson then kicked him in the head. More confused now by the violent assault, Frykowski asked, "Who are you?" to which Watson replied, "I'm the devil and I'm here to do the devil's business."

Atkins then walked down the hallway past Abigail Folger's room, and Folger waved at her thinking it was somebody else. Atkins stopped, went back into Folger's room, and, at knife point, brought her out and sat her next to Frykowski. Atkins then went back and rounded up Tate and Sebring and took them out to the living room with the others.

Once Tate, Sebring, Frykowski, and Folger were together, Watson tied a rope around Sebring's neck, tossed the rope over a ceiling beam and then tied the other end around Tate's neck. Jay Sebring had already complained to the four about the rough treatment of a pregnant Tate, and he again spoke up. This time, without a word, Watson pointed the pistol at Sebring and shot him. He then kicked him repeatedly and stabbed him. This act made it clear that the intruders where going to kill them. Frykowski had his hands tied with a towel and managed to free himself. As he started to run, Atkins attempted to stop him, and they began wrestling with each other until Frykowski broke away and headed for the door. Watson now turned away from the killing of Sebring and gave chase; he tackled him and began beating him over the head with the butt end of the pistol breaking the grip in the process. Watson then stood up and shot Frykowski. Back inside the home, Abigail Folger and Krenwinkel were struggling with each other, and Krenwinkel had already managed to stab her multiple times, none of which were fatal. Folger briefly got free and made her way out of a bedroom window and headed for the front lawn. Krenwinkel caught up with her and stabbed and kicked her until Watson came over and helped finish the deed. Watson then returned to Frykowski and continued to stab him until he was dead.

Sharon Tate remained tied up while the melee ensued pleading with Susan Atkins to let her child live. Atkins response to Tate's appeal was, "Shut up bitch; I don't care about your baby." Tex Watson and Patricia Krenwinkel were now back in the house, and Watson went back to Jay Sebring and plunged the knife into him a few more times to be sure he was dead. Then he and Atkins began stabbing Sharon Tate. While they were stabbing her, Tate kept asking for her mother until she took her last breath. Before leaving the scene, Atkins gathered up the towel they had used to tie Frykowski's hands and soaked it in Sharon Tate's blood, she then went to the front door and using the blood soaked towel wrote the word, "pig" in big letters. Steven Parent, Jay Sebring, Abigail Folger, Wojciech Frykowski, Sharon Tate and her unborn son, Paul Richard Polanski, died August 9, 1969.

The next morning when the horrific events were discovered, it was found that Steven Parent had been sliced with a knife and shot four times, Jay Sebring had been shot and then stabbed seven times, Abigail Folger had twenty-eight stab wounds, and Wojciech Frykowski had been shot twice and then been stabbed fifty-one times. Perhaps the most horrific of the murders was the pregnant Sharon Tate: she had been stabbed sixteen times, five of which would have been fatal wounds, and her unborn child had received many of the knife wounds as well. Tate was found still connected to Sebring by the rope around both of their necks. The police took the caretaker, William Garretson, into custody for the murders, but he was later released after he passed a polygraph test. The news reported that morning that, other than Garretson, they had, "No other suspects at this time."

Upon hearing the news reports and having been told all that had occurred that night by the four murderers, Manson was upset that it hadn't had the required affect on the population. He also deemed the murders sloppy and was disappointed by the lack of panic it caused. He told his followers that another example had to be made that evening and that he himself would go along to, "show them how to do it." That night, August 10, Manson, Leslie Van Houten, Patricia Krenwinkel, Charles "Tex" Watson, Susan Atkins, Linda Kasabian, and Steve "Clem" Grogan left Spahn Ranch headed for Beverly Hills. After driving around for a couple of hours looking for the right place to do the deed, Manson directed them to 3301 Waverly Drive in Los Feliz. This was the home of supermarket owner Leno LaBianca and his wife, Rosemary; Manson remembered this house from a party he had attended at one of their neighbor's and now realized that a gruesome murder in the affluent neighborhood would be the perfect place to breed fear and panic.

When the group arrived at the house, Manson got out and told the rest to wait in the car until he returned; he then disappeared up the driveway. Manson returned a few minutes later, and he and Watson went back up to the house. There, Manson woke the sleeping Leno LaBianca from the couch and had Watson tie his hands; they then went to the bedroom, brought out Rosemary, and bound her hands, and ordered Tex to put pillow cases over their heads. Manson kept telling the LaBiancas that they were just there to rob them and that they weren't going to be hurt. Charlie then left to get Patricia Krenwinkel and Leslie Van Houten, bringing them up to the house. He told the girls to go into the kitchen to look for "tools" they could use for the job at hand. Manson then left the house.

Manson and his followers stole into this home and
brutally killed Rosemary and Leno LaBianca.

Tex Watson now ordered Krenwinkel and Van Houten into the bedroom with orders to kill Rosemary LaBianca. Watson headed back out to the living room and stabbed Leno in the throat; he continued to stab him twelve times. While Watson was taking care of Leno, Krenwinkel and Van Houten were having trouble with Rosemary in the bedroom. Rosemary had gotten free enough that she could swing the lamp that was attached to the cord around her neck, and she was keeping the two women at bay with it. Watson heard the commotion and hurriedly went to the bedroom and stabbed Rosemary several times. Rosemary crumpled to the floor, and Watson then went back out to finish off Leno. After Leno was dead, Tex Watson carved the word "War" into Leno LaBianca's stomach with his knife.

Heading back to the bedroom, Watson saw that Krenwinkel was busy stabbing Rosemary, but Van Houten was just standing there watching. Manson had told Tex that he wanted to make sure that each of the women "played their part" in the killings, and so he directed Van Houten to stab Rosemary LaBianca as well. Leslie Van Houten then repeatedly stabbed Rosemary in the back and buttocks sixteen times. In all, Rosemary LaBianca was stabbed forty-one times. After the three killers left the bedroom, Patricia Krenwinkel went to the kitchen and wrote the word, "Rise" on one wall, "Death to pigs" on another, and then, on the refrigerator door misspelled, "Healter (sic) Skelter," all of it written in the blood of Leno and Rosemary LaBianca. Krenwinkel then went to a drawer, grabbed a two-tine carving fork and stabbed Leno with it seven times, finally leaving it imbedded in his stomach. She also left a steak knife sticking out of Leno's throat.

After the gruesome killings, Watson, Krenwinkel, and Van Houten showered and then made themselves at home in the kitchen. The girls went about making a dinner of sandwiches and salad along with wine they had found there and sat down at the kitchen table to enjoy their meal. This act shows just how disconnected from humanity those who followed Charles Manson had become. After they were finished with dinner, the three casually left their bloody mess for the LaBianca family to discover the next day. Leno and Rosemary LaBianca died August 10, 1969.

Shortly after the horrific murders, the police raided Spahn Ranch. Bobby Beausoleil had already been arrested in the Hinman murder, and the Los Angeles police and Los Angeles sheriffs had no solid leads or suspects in the Tate/LaBianca murders, so the raid on August 16 had nothing to do with the Manson killings; it was all due to car thefts in the area. The police found the large cache of weapons that the group had stockpiled, along with parts from the many Volkswagens that had been stolen and turned into dune buggies. Manson and the rest of the family present that day were arrested, but due to some errors made, they were released without being charged.

Charlie knew that many of the hired hands on Spahn Ranch disliked him and knew as well that they wanted the family gone. One in particular had always been vocal about it and Manson knew that he had gone to George Spahn and all but demanded that Spahn tell Manson to get out. Now, Manson figured, that person, Donald "Shorty" Shea, had tried to get around the problem by calling the police himself with the hopes that they would force the family to leave. Manson had always disliked Shea because Donald's ex-wife was a black woman and Manson was a firm believer in not mixing the races. Now, with the belief that Shea had "snitched" on the family, Manson gave the order to have him killed.

Manson told Tex Watson, Bruce Davis, and Steve Grogan to ask Shea for a ride to a nearby car parts yard and then while in the car they were to kill him. The three men asked Shea to stop by the side of the road, near a tree where Manson always came to play his guitar, so they could pick something up for Charlie. As soon as Shea stopped the car, Grogan, who was sitting in the back seat with Davis, hit Shea over the head with a pipe wrench and Watson stabbed him. They then dragged Shea from the car and down a hill below what is now called the "Manson Tree" and tortured him to death. Bruce Davis later recalled, "I was in the back seat when Grogan hit him and Charles Watson stabbed him. They took Shorty out . . . they had to go down the hill to a place, and I stayed in the car. I went down the hill later on, and that's when I cut Shorty on the shoulder with the knife . . ."

This tree is where Manson would play his guitar for his family and where Donald "Shorty" Shea was brought to be killed.

The brutality of this murder can be summed up in the Grand Jury testimony of family member Barbara Hoyt, "It was about 10:00 p.m. when I heard a long, loud, blood-curdling scream. Then it went quiet for a minute or so, and then the screams came again and again; it seemed to go on forever. I have no doubt that Shorty was being murdered at that time."

After Shea was finally dead, Grogan buried him on the hill just above the railroad tracks that ran through the pass. On December 9, 1969, Donald Shea's 1962 Mercury was found; inside was a footlocker filled with Shorty's possessions, a pair of bloodstained cowboy boots belonging to him, and on top of the footlocker's lid was a clear palm print belonging to Bruce Davis. There was a rumor that Donald Shea had been dismembered into nine pieces and decapitated. Where this rumor began is also grounds for speculation; however, when Shea's body was finally found intact in December of 1977, the rumor was dispelled once and for all. Donald "Shorty" Shea was killed on August 26, 1969.

Soon after Shea was murdered, Manson and his family moved back out to Barker Ranch in Death Valley and began preparing for Helter Skelter. There is much speculation that while the cult was there, they committed a few more murders: Those unlucky enough to come across their preparations and those members who refused to tow the line are said to be buried near the ranch, but no proof has ever surfaced, so it remains unclear if there is any validity to the rumors. Once settled in at Barker and Myers Ranches, the family began looking for entrances that could be used to find the "Bottomless Pit" that would lay the groundwork for the city that Manson had envisioned. During one of these excursions, members destroyed an earthmover they found—they did not know or did not care that the piece of equipment was still in use by the Death Valley National Monument. On October 12, 1969, a joint task force of National Park Rangers, Inyo County Sheriffs, and Highway Patrol swiftly raided the ranches and arrested everyone there. Charles Manson was found hiding in the tiny cabinet under the sink of the cabin at Barker Ranch.

The police were still unaware that the gruesome murders were committed by Manson and his followers; it would take another month to piece together the evidence and then only because Susan Atkins could not keep quiet about her exploits while in Sybil Brand Detention Center awaiting trial on other charges. On June 15, 1970, Manson, Watson, Atkins, and Krenwinkel were charged, each with seven counts of murder and one count of conspiracy to commit murder. Kasabian was granted immunity for her testimony and was never charged. Leslie Van Houten was charged with two counts of murder and one count of conspiracy to commit murder.

The trial became a media circus: Family members would hold "sit ins" outside the courthouse; inside the courtroom, Charles Manson had carved an X into his forehead in protest at being removed as his own counsel, and now many of his followers followed suit. Manson was constantly

The culvert where Shea was tossed while he slowly died.

disrupting testimony in defiance of his lawyer, and other family members attempted to dissuade witnesses by threatening them. One witness, Paul Watkins, was badly burned in a suspicious fire that started while he was in his van. Barbara Hoyt, a former family member and a key prosecution witness, accompanied Ruth Ann Moorehouse to Hawaii during a break in the trial, and while there, Moorehouse gave Hoyt a hamburger laced with overdose amounts of LSD and then grabbed a quick flight back to Los Angeles. Luckily, Hoyt managed to crawl into a Honolulu hospital where they were able to save her life. Family members Mary Brunner, Catherine Share, Lawrence Brunner, Dennis Rice, and Kenneth Cole even tried to rob a surplus store of guns and ammo in an attempt to highjack an airliner; their idea was to shoot one passenger every hour until Manson was released from jail. The attempt failed when Hawthorne Police came upon the scene and, after a brief shoot out, took the five into custody.

The biggest mystery surrounding the trial of Manson and his cult followers is that of Ronald Hughes. Hughes was Leslie Van Houten's attorney during the Tate/LaBianca murder trial. He had actually been the first lawyer to speak with Charlie Manson, but his inexperience caused him to be replaced before the trial began, and he was appointed counsel for Van Houten instead. Hughes tried to separate Van Houten from Manson by showing that his client had no control over her actions and that Manson had brainwashed her so completely that Van Houten would do anything Manson asked without question. This tactic almost certainly got the man killed. While out camping in late November of 1970, during a court break, Ronald Hughes disappeared without a trace. It was suspected that other family members had killed him on Manson's orders, but to this day, no one has been arrested in connection with the crime, even though family members were heard saying that it was a retaliation murder ordered by Manson. Hughes' badly decomposed body was found in late March 1971.

In a separate trial in 1971, Manson was found guilty in the murders of Gary Hinman and Donald Shea. Also in separate trials, Charles "Tex" Watson and Steve "Clem" Grogan were found guilty of Shea's murder. Susan Atkins was found guilty in the murder of Gary Hinman. Mary Brunner testified for the prosecution in the Hinman case against Bobby Beausoleil and was granted immunity but was then arrested in the attempted robbery of the Western Surplus store in Hawthorne, California.

THE BREAKDOWN:

Charles "Tex" Watson: Convicted on seven counts of murder, life in prison.
Susan Atkins: Convicted on seven counts of murder, life in prison. Atkins died September 24, 2009.
Robert Beausoleil: Convicted on one count of murder, life in prison.
Leslie Van Houten: Convicted on two counts of murder, life in prison.
Steve "Clem" Grogan: Convicted on one count of murder, life in prison.
Patricia Krenwinkel: Convicted on seven counts of murder, life in prison.
Bruce Davis: Convicted on two counts of murder, life in prison.

Linda Kasabian: Indicted for the Tate/LaBianca murders, Kasabian turned State's witness and was granted immunity. She was last seen living in abject poverty out of the public eye.

Charles Manson: Convicted on seven counts of murder plus one count each for Hinman and Shea, life in prison.

Charles Manson and his family have worked their way into the fabric of Americana with the brutal murders of innocent people; there have been numerous movies about their exploits and documentaries attempting to explain what occurred and why. Myths have grown around the ranches where they lived, and TV has even begun creating fiction about Charlie and his cult as a way of bringing them into their shows. Charles Manson never actually killed anyone that we know of, although he tried to kill one man, Bernard Crowe, but was unsuccessful. However, Vincent Bugliosi, lead prosecutor in the trial believes that Manson may have actually killed more than thirty-six people over the course of the family's reign of terror. His hold over his followers was absolute, and because of this, Manson is responsible for at least nine deaths, including that of an unborn infant. There may be more yet to be discovered in Death Valley, but the way that Manson told his family to kill the innocents was brutal beyond any form of humanity, and to this author, it makes Charles Manson one of the most evil people to ever walk this Earth.

PARANORMAL ASSOCIATION

It is said that violence can be the reason for a person's spirit to remain behind after they have died. In the case of Manson and his family I can think of no crimes more heinous, more violent and cruel than those committed by Watson, Atkins, Krenwinkel, and the others on Manson's orders. What makes this whole tale even more eerie is that Sharon Tate may have known what was going to happen to her before it occurred, if only she had listened.

Three years before the gruesome killings, Sharon Tate was between apartments and needed a place to stay for a couple of days. She had dated Jay Sebring and knowing that he had just bought a house in Benedict Canyon had asked if she could stay there until she found her own place; Jay readily agreed and Sharon moved in. The home once belonged to Jean Harlow and Paul Bern and is where Bern committed suicide, or so they think. This home was less than a mile from where Sharon would later be killed.

Jay Sebring was out of town, and Sharon was alone in the house. She had been getting a strange vibe all night but had chalked it up to her being by herself and had

The area "Shorty" Shea's body was finally recovered.

tried to put it out of her mind. She was in bed trying to fall asleep; she had left a light on next to the bed and suddenly noticed a "creepy little man" enter the bedroom. Sharon recognized the man from pictures Sebring had shown her of the previous owner; it was Paul Bern. Bern seemed to be looking for something; Tate had no idea what it could be but wasn't about to wait around to find out. Sharon grabbed a robe and bolted for the door to make her way downstairs. Once there, however, she wished she had stayed in her room. What greeted her at the bottom of the landing was the sight of a person; she couldn't tell if it was male or female but they were tied to the staircase with their throat slit open.

At this point, Sharon was almost frantic and needed a drink. She had no idea where Jay kept the liquor, but something told her to open the bookcase. Inside she found a hidden bar and poured herself a drink. While she sipped, she glanced around and noticed some wallpaper and began to pick at it, finally uncovering a beautiful copper base to the bar. Thinking she must be dreaming, Sharon walked back upstairs past the body tied to the railing, past the ghost of Paul Bern and somehow went to sleep.

The next morning dawned bright and clear, and as Sharon woke up, the visions of the night before were still fresh in her mind. Again, she told herself that it had only been a dream, that she had not seen a ghost or anything else she had thought she had seen. As she got out of bed, she heard Jay Sebring come through the front door; as she was about to head down the stairs, she heard him call up and say, "Hey, who tore the wallpaper off the bar down here?" That's when Sharon Tate realized it had not been just a dream.

Three years later, Tate and Sebring would be tied together with ropes, just as the apparition had been, they would be brutally stabbed and killed, just as the apparition had been, all just a mile up the road. Could this have been Paul Bern's way of trying to warn Sharon of the danger that awaited her? Could this have been her own precognitive ability that had somehow manifested itself to try to save her? Or was it just a cosmic coincidence? Unfortunately, we will never know.

At the house in Malibu where Gary Hinman was tortured and murdered, former residents have reported the sounds of chanting at all hours of the day and night. There doesn't seem to be any time that it occurs more frequently, and the duration of the chanting varies significantly. What is strange about this is that it sounds as if it should be a residual haunting but does not follow the normal strictures of this type of activity. Residual hauntings are an imprint in time from a highly emotional type of death. In the case of Gary Hinman, it would have been caused by his brutal murder. However, a residual occurs at the same time and place every time; in the case of the chanting this is not happening. Could this be Hinman himself still practicing his Buddhism when he has the time in his afterlife?

Another strange story I came across dealt with a television that once belonged to Hinman at the time of his murder. It seems that a young lady was staying at her sister's house very near where Hinman was killed. She had been doing laundry alone when she heard static coming from an old TV. She went to investigate and found the television in a storage room turned on but to a channel that was off-air and blaring out white noise. As this woman switched the TV off and turned to leave, she noticed a face staring back at her through the static. As it turns out, a family member had purchased the television from the Hinman estate following the murder, and what this young lady saw that day may have been the ghost of Gary Hinman calling out from the grave.

Spahn Ranch is situated in Chatsworth, California, in the Santa Susana Pass. The ranch was home to the Manson family for some time and is the place where stuntman and ranch hand Donald "Shorty" Shea was murdered by the cult. There have been reports of Shea's spirit roaming the old ranch site even to this day.

The "back" entrance to the Cielo Drive house. It was not in existence at the time of the murders.

Shea was killed following the Tate/LaBianca murders, and his body was buried on the ranch until police located him eight years later. Reports from the area include the sound of laughter suddenly erupting on car radios, even if they are switched off. This happens mostly at night but has been known to occur at all hours. The sound of the laughter has been said to be that of a male with a deep voice, and it only happens while passing the ranch itself. As soon as the car is past where the buildings used to sit, the laughter stops, and the radio again functions properly. There have also been numerous reports from people visiting the area of a headless man seen standing high up on a hilltop just gazing down at them; as they watch, the figure will simply fade from sight as if it had never been. This same figure has been seen, although on very rare occasions, wandering the area where the buildings of the old west movie town had been located before being destroyed by fire. Again, the figure will stay visible for a short time and then fade away. It is believed that this solitary spirit is that of Donald "Shorty" Shea.

Perhaps the strangest reports from the area involve something that may have no connection with Manson and his cult whatsoever; the tales revolve around a specter known as "The Watcher." The reports almost always begin at or near the Ranch and end just after passing the property line. People driving by will report seeing a 1960s sedan suddenly appear in their rearview mirror, and it will begin tailgating them. If the driver speeds up, the sedan speeds up as well; if the driver pulls over and stops, the sedan does also. It is one of those things that frightens you no matter who you are. No one ever exits the sedan, and no one can be seen behind the wheel due to dirt covering the windshield; however, in every instance, as soon as the unsuspecting driver passes the old Spahn Movie Ranch, the sedan suddenly and mysteriously vanishes. What or who "The Watcher" is no one knows. Because the sedan is from the 1960s and always appears near the Manson family hideout, some believe it is somehow connected and is some of Manson's deceased followers keeping people from the ranch.

Another place where Manson and his cult of killers hid out was the Barker Ranch in Death Valley. Even though there has never been proof of any killings there, family member Susan Atkins has said that there are many bodies buried in and around the ranch. These range from other family members who tried to leave Manson, as well as those just unlucky enough to come across the cult while hiking. Cadaver dogs from the Sheriff's Department have picked up telltale signs, but as of yet, no concrete evidence has been located. There have been reports of spirit activity at the location, however. Over the years, many people have camped overnight at the Barker Ranch; tales have been told of waking up from a deep sleep to the sounds of howling. The sound is not that of coyotes but that of human beings suffering. Could this be the sound of those Manson had tortured and killed to keep from leaving the fold? Others have claimed to see apparitions out of the corners of their eyes, and still others have alleged to have actually been touched by unseen hands. One extreme case centers around two men who had gone there to see where Manson was finally captured. Upon entering what was left of the cabin, one of the men heard a low growl and felt a slicing pain run down his back. He quickly left and found his friend who inspected the man's back to find what appeared to be three animal scratches running from shoulder to buttocks.

Perhaps the most compelling stories of the paranormal in regards to the Manson killings come from the home of David Oman. This gentleman lives on Cielo Drive just a stone's throw from where Sharon Tate, Jay Sebring, and three others were brutally murdered by Manson's followers. Shortly after Oman moved into his house, he began to notice strange things occurring inside the luxury home. At one point he thought he saw someone in his house but soon realized that they appeared wispy and insubstantial. He began to believe that they may be spirits but who the spirits were he was unsure. He decided to do a bit of digging into his home's history and came across a picture of Jay Sebring and recognized him as the person he had seen in his house. Oman soon realized that what he was seeing in his home were the spirits of the murder victims from the home up the street. Over the years, he has found that it was not just Sebring who was trying to make themselves known but Sharon Tate as well. It would seem that they may have unfinished business or are just trying to make sure that they are not forgotten. Perhaps they want to make sure people remember them as they were and not only as the victims that most people know them to be.

Oman is not shy about letting people know his home is haunted—on the contrary, he has openly embraced his guests and has even given them an outlet for trying to get their message out to the world. Mr. Oman has opened his house to people who have a desire to investigate the unknown, and his property has never failed to give these adventurers what they are looking for. Renowned paranormalist Dr. Barry Taff, who became famous for his investigation of the "Entity" case, was the first to document the activity within the home. He recorded so much activity that he called the house, "the Mount Everest of haunted houses" and "the Disneyland for the dead."

Mr. Oman has never been apprehensive about the ghostly visitors in his home; in his view they are just guests. He once said: "I always felt that I wasn't alone here . . . I'm way more scared of the living than the dead." Every few months, David Oman opens his house to the curious for investigation, and it would seem from the reports of those brave enough to participate that Dr. Taff and Mr. Oman have not over stated their nicknames for the home. I am sure that the spirits are thankful that they have a place where they can be remembered and where the evils of the past can stay known in the hopes that we can keep them from happening again in the future.

Charles Manson may have been one of the most evil and devious men to ever be born; he ranks right up there with Adolph Hitler and Josef Stalin—not in the numbers of people he murdered but in the intent of his crimes. One wonders how many more victims remain in the desert waiting to be found or how many more Manson and his cult would have killed if he had not been apprehended when he was. Suffice it to say that the world is much better off with Manson and his murderous followers in prison. Let us all hope that they never win parole and will pass from this existence while still behind bars.

CHAPTER 10

NATALIE WOOD

Natalie Wood's Walk of Fame star at 7000 Hollywood Boulevard. (Notice the piece of wood left by a fan.)

Hollywood marriages always seem to be the stuff that dreams are made of; at least, they are made to look that way by the trade magazines and the media who follow the famous couple everywhere they go and do their best to make us all wish we were the ones living their fairy tale lives. This was the case for more than twenty-five years with Natalie Wood and her on-again off-again husband, Robert Wagner. Their first marriage ended in just six years, but they remarried and seemed to be living the life we all want—love, fame, riches, they had it all, and people followed their lives as if they were their own close friends. What happens when that ideal existence is suddenly shattered by a mysterious death? A death that may be from murder brought on by an icon we have loved and dreamed about, an idol brought low by scandal and suspicion, and the other idol brought down in death and mourning?

Born Natalia Nikolaevna Zakharenko in San Francisco, California, in 1938, to Russian immigrant parents, young Natalie grew up in an abusive household to a mother, Maria, who was determined to have her daughter become a wealthy actress so Natalia could provide the lavish lifestyle she demanded in life. Not satisfied with what her husband was providing for her, Maria divorced Nikolai and she soon met and married Nicholas Gurdin, who adopted Natalia just before he moved the family from San Francisco to Santa Rosa, California, just a few miles away. (There are persistent rumors that Maria and Nikolai continued having an affair after the divorce, which lasted until his death.) Gurdin was basically a good man; however, he was a drunk and would fly into fits of rage while drinking. This made young Natalia terrified of his bouts, but otherwise she loved him as any daughter would her father.

It was while they lived in Santa Rosa that Natalia, or one could say Maria, got her big break. Natalia's mother really didn't care which one of her daughters became the star in the family as long as one of them made it big. So one day, while Maria and the girls were at the park, she noticed that there was filming going on and ordered five-year-old Natalia to go and sit on director Irving Pichel's lap. Pichel was surprised by the gesture but also captivated by the child's looks and immediately gave her a walk-on role to test her screen presence; her older half-sister Olga also had a walk-on role. It wasn't long before Maria had the family moving to Los Angeles where she began to groom Natalia and where the connections she made that day in the park were fully utilized.

Wood's debut role was in 1945 opposite Orson Welles and Claudette Colbert in the film *Tomorrow Is Forever*. In the movie Natalie Wood (Irving Pichel, who directed this film had Natalie change her name to something less "communist" sounding,) played a German orphan, and Welles would later state: "She is a born professional, so good she was terrifying." Maria was thrilled that her daughter had broken into the film industry, and young Natalie was now her meal ticket. Her mother was relentless in pushing Natalie into more and more roles over the next eight years; she appeared in sixteen movies and three television shows. Maria had complete control; she wouldn't even let Natalie see or answer her own fan mail. Her mother even used Natalie's influence to get her husband a job working as a carpenter at 20th Century Fox studios, although she wanted it kept a secret from all but family. One instance that Maria called "quite embarrassing," was when Natalie's father entered the set she was working on and she happily and loudly called out, "Daddy!" When Maria found out what Natalie had done, she vehemently chastised her daughter for embarrassing her like that and forbade her from ever acknowledging her father on the studio grounds again. As a child actor, young Natalie Wood distinguished herself as a star in films such as *Miracle on 34th Street* and *The Ghost and Mrs. Muir*. Natalie Wood, unlike most actors, managed to transition from child star to adult actor almost flawlessly.

One of Wood's most remembered films, and also her first as an "adult," was the teen angst movie *Rebel Without a Cause*. Natalie was only sixteen and starred opposite James Dean, Sal Mineo, and Dennis Hopper. In a strange twist of fate, all of the stars in that movie, other than Hopper, met a tragic death. Natalie Wood went on to star in many standout roles in the early 1960s, such as *West Side Story, Love With the Proper Stranger, Splendor in the Grass, Gypsy,* and *Bob & Carol & Ted & Alice.*

While growing up with an abusive mother and alcoholic father, Natalie was always looking for ways to escape her troubles. Music had always been one way in which she accomplished this, but then she met flamboyant, bi-sexual Nicholas Ray while testing for her part in *Rebel Without a Cause.* The same day sixteen-year-old Natalie met Ray, she lost her virginity. This set her on a roller coaster ride of men that would last until the day she died. At first Natalie tried to keep her affairs secret. She would slip off the set with Dennis Hopper or quietly sneak men into her room at home when her mother was away, and even though her mother knew, as long as her daughter kept bringing in the money, she remained silent. That is until Natalie met Robert Wagner, known as R. J.

Wood had originally met Robert Wagner when she was ten years old on the Fox studio lot; she fell instantly in love with the nineteen-year-old actor. The family was living in Laurel Canyon when filming began on *Rebel*, and Natalie's sister was quoted as saying in her book *Natalie: A Memoir by Her Sister*, "Boys flowed in and out of our house, and every arrival and departure and everything in between was carefully monitored by Mother." In 1957, Natalie was again introduced to Robert Wagner, and the two became inseparable. Maria loved R. J. as well and allowed Wagner to sleep in the same room with Natalie—not only at home but also in public hotels during movie shoots. Later that year, Wagner proposed, and they were married three weeks later.

Even though R. J. and Natalie's marriage was short lived and they divorced in 1962, they still loved each other—but living together was impossible for both of them. Natalie would later say that she was just too young and could not make it work. Over the next decade, Natalie would have a series of affairs: Warren Beatty, Nicky Hilton, and Frank Sinatra among them. She met and fell in love with British agent/producer Richard Gregson, whom she married in 1969, and they had a daughter, Natasha. She divorced him in 1972; this same year, Natalie and Wagner reconciled and remarried. Wood and R. J. had a daughter, Courtney, in 1974, and Natalie decided to put her career on hold to raise her two children.

Even though Wood had decided to take a break from movies to raise her kids, she knew that if she ever wanted to return to the big screen, she would have to keep her foot in the door. With this in mind, she took several television roles; these included, *The Cracker Factory, From Here to Eternity,* and her last completed project, *The Memory of Eva Ryker*. She turned down a few movie roles knowing that the time needed to complete the films would keep her away from her family for more time than she was willing to give. Some of these titles were, *Goodbye Columbus, The Great Gatsby,* and *The Towering Inferno*.

When her daughters reached school age, Natalie decided it was time to throw her hat back into the ring; she had heard about a film project touted as "a technological masterpiece" and directed by Douglas Trumbull, who had made a name for himself with the blockbuster movies, *2001: A Space Odyssey* and *Close Encounters of the Third*

Kind. Wood jumped at the opportunity to appear in the film and was immediately cast playing Christopher Walken's estranged wife in the movie *Brainstorm* in 1981.

Almost as soon as filming began, rumors began to surface of an affair between Walken and Wood; they both denied the allegations, and as Wagner, Wood, and Walken became friends, R. J. never brought up the subject—that is until the night of November 29, 1981. Natalie and R. J. had gotten into the habit of spending Thanksgiving on their yacht, *Splendor*, at Two Harbors on Catalina Island; they had decided to invite Walken for the holiday as a way for the three of them to unwind from a busy movie and TV schedule.

Even though Wagner never said anything about an affair, he had his suspicions. In his 2008 memoirs Wagner stated: "She was more involved with the movie than she was with her family, and the thought occurred to me that Natalie was being emotionally unfaithful." It would all come to a head on the night Natalie died.

The evening of November 28 found Walken and Wood in the bar at Doug's Harbor Reef, the only restaurant at the Isthmus of Two Harbors; R. J. had decided to lie down for a bit, and when he fell asleep, the other two had decided to start the evening without him. When Wagner awoke a few hours later and found the two gone, he was upset and immediately headed to the bar to find them. By the time he met up with Wood and Walken, his anger had died down, and the three of them went into the dining room to have dinner. While eating, they ordered a few bottles of champagne as well as mixed drinks, and by the time the evening was over, they needed help getting back to the *Splendor*. Doug Bombard, the owner of the restaurant later said: "My assistant manager was seeing that they got out. To make sure they got on the boat okay." Bombard would later find the body of Natalie Wood floating in the cove near his restaurant.

After Wood, R. J., and Walken arrived back on the *Splendor*, the drinking continued, and at some point, the topic turned to how much time should be spent on a career compared to time given to the actor's family. R. J. thought that his wife was not taking her responsibilities to her family as seriously as she should and believed that her filming schedule should be shortened. Walken took Natalie's side in the argument, which sent Wagner into a rage. R. J. then picked up a wine bottle and smashed it over a table; he then brandished the jagged glass at Walken saying: " Do you want to fuck my wife?" Walken casually stood up, said goodnight, and retired to his cabin.

After Walken went to bed, Wood and Wagner began to argue heatedly, their anger fueled by the copious amounts of alcohol they had consumed. Up on the bridge of the yacht, Captain Dennis Davern heard the commotion but decided not to intervene. He knew that Natalie and R. J. had been arguing all weekend and figured that it was just another of the couple's fights. He stated that he couldn't make out what the two were saying but clearly heard R. J. when he yelled for Natalie to "get off my fucking boat!" After this statement the yacht became quiet again. A short time later, Davern came down to the main deck to find Wagner at the stern of the boat looking "sweaty, flushed, anxious, nervous, and disheveled." Wagner, once he realized that Davern had come up behind him said, "Natalie is missing."

Once it became known that Wood was not on the *Splendor*, Davern wanted to immediately radio for help and turn on the searchlights. Wagner, however, told him no and said that they would wait to see if she would return. The captain thought this was a bit odd but agreed to R. J.'s wishes. While they waited on deck, Wagner opened a bottle of scotch and the two men drank, Wagner refilling Davern's glass as soon as he noticed it was empty. Davern has stated publicly that he knew he should have done more to help Natalie but listened to Wagner because they had been friends for so long. It wasn't until the next morning that Natalie's body was found by the man who'd had his employees help her and her companions back to the yacht, Dave Bombard.

Natalie Wood's imprints at Grauman's Chinese Theater.

Bombard was on his way to the restaurant when he noticed something bright red floating in the water; as he took a closer look, he realized that it was a body. "She was just hanging, her feet down . . . her face down. Her hair was all over, but still a beautiful gal." Bombard said that he found Natalie floating straight up and down, her red down jacket keeping her body from sinking. "She was a beautiful woman, even in death," said Bombard. Bombard broke the news to R. J., and he said that when Wagner heard that his wife's body had been found, Wagner looked as if he already knew she was dead. ". . . I don't think it was news [to Wagner]; he looked down," said Bombard.

The police investigation of the case and the coroner's report stated that the cause of death was "accident by drowning and hypothermia." The autopsy noted a blood alcohol level of 0.14 percent with traces of two types of medication, a motion-sickness drug and painkillers. Thomas Noguchi stated that it appeared that "Ms. Wood had been drinking and may have slipped while trying to re-board the dinghy." This goes along with the sworn testimony of Wagner, Walken, and Davern. Noguchi was demoted a year later after an internal investigation exposed him as a media-hungry opportunist who would change reports for the sole purpose of seeking publicity after celebrity deaths.

Speculation at the time, be it rumor or a need for fans to have an excuse for an idol's death, had Robert Wagner killing his wife over her affair with Walken and the many more that came before. Wagner was never a suspect as far as the police were concerned, but that still hasn't stopped the rumors even to this day. Whether they truly are just rumors, there are still many unanswered questions that remain, and now, after all of these years, Captain Davern has come out with some truly strange tales about that night and even more questions that need to be answered.

One of the things that had been glossed over in the coroner's report and the media were the bruises found on Natalie's body. These bruises were mostly consistent with a possible fall from the boat, but others were a bit more suspicious. There were fresh bruises on her left wrist that looked as if they were defensive; Natalie also had bruising on the left side of her forehead as well as a fresh scratch on the back of her neck. Her body showed signs of bruising on the back of both legs, too; there were some that appeared to be a day or more old. All of these were inconsistent with a fall into the water. They were all also left out of the original coroner's report.

Another strange twist has to do with Wagner's reluctance to immediately radio for help and his refusal to turn on a search light. It seems odd that he would be so cavalier where the life of his wife may have been in jeopardy. The coroner's report states that Wagner told them he found his wife missing around 11:45 p.m.; however, his radio call wasn't heard until 1:30 a.m., almost two hours later. Rodger Smith, a former Los Angeles County rescue boat captain and one of the men who helped recover Natalie's body, told the LA Times that he hoped the reopening of the case would answer lingering questions about the time delay in notifying the life guards that Natalie was missing. Smith believes that from the looks of the body, Wood had been alive for quite some time in the water and probably cried out for help for hours. This ties in with one of the witness's claims that she heard Wood crying for help. Retired stockbroker, Marilyn Wayne, who was on another yacht the night that Natalie went missing, said she heard the movie star's "last desperate cries for help." She also said that police had refused to listen to her evidence. It seems unlikely that with at least three people on other yachts nearby who said that they heard someone calling for help that those on the *Splendor* couldn't hear her pleas as well.

Perhaps the strangest accusation comes from the *Splendor's* Captain Davern. At the time of the incident, Davern's statements exactly matched those of Wagner; however, Davern is now saying that Wagner told him what to say. "He discussed with me the repercussions of bringing immediate attention to the situation, and he claimed he did not want to tarnish his image." Davern has now come forward with "new" information that has caused the case to be reopened.

No one outside of those on the *Splendor* knows what really happened that night, and other than Davern, they are staying with the story they told the police the morning of November 29, 1981. Some believe that Natalie was trying to escape the arguments that had taken place earlier that evening and were continuing still on the yacht; others say that she was just trying to tie up the loose dinghy to stop it from banging on the side of the boat and was keeping her from getting to sleep. Still others will always believe that R. J. pushed her into the water knowing full well that Natalie had a dreadful, childhood fear of dying in "dark water." Wagner knew that once in the ocean her fear would most likely do the job of killing her. Whatever the actual truth of the death of Natalie Wood is, it seems that she cannot rest in peace; it appears that she has something yet to say as her spirit has been seen in more than one place.

PARANORMAL ASSOCIATION

Natalie Wood's final resting place at Westwood Village Memorial Park. She is buried near Marilyn Monroe.

Natalie Wood was loved by millions of fans; on the morning of November 29, 1981, those fans awoke to a nightmare: their idol, Natalie Wood, was dead. Almost immediately the rumors and suspicions spread around the world: Her husband, Robert Wagner, broke her neck and tried to hide the body in the water; Christopher Walken murdered her because she wouldn't leave her husband and continue their affair; there was even an obtuse rumor involving organized crime and Frank Sinatra. But whatever the actual truth may be, Natalie, it would seem, is trying to get her tale told even after her untimely death.

The *Splendor* was sold in 1986 to a retired flight attendant, Ron Nelson, who had dreams of sailing it to Hawaii and turning it into a charter yacht for tourists. Almost from day one the new owner began to notice strange things occurring on his acquired vessel. Never one prone to falls, he found that while on board he would hit the deck for no discernable reason: "It's just like my feet came out from under me and I fell." He said that the falls occurred while the boat was tied up at the dock, so motion was never really a factor. Nelson has told of seeing shadows out of the corners of his eyes, but they are gone when he looks directly in the shadow's direction. He says that it looks like a woman and that she is simply staring at him. Once, while sailing the yacht to Honolulu, he went to bed late one night, and while he was lying there, he felt someone sit down on the bed next to him. Who or whatever it was sat there for a few moments and then rose from the bed and left. This incident convinced Nelson to have the *Splendor* blessed as soon as he arrived in Hawaii. Once he arrived in port, he sought out two Kahunas, Hawaiian shaman, and had them perform a "cleaning" ritual on the yacht. Nelson said that it failed to remove the spirit from the yacht, however. Nelson now firmly believes that the ghost haunting his ship is that of Natalie Wood.

Over the years, Nelson has tried to live with the strange goings on but has grown tired of having to deal with the sudden falls he believes are caused by Natalie's spirit. He has been injured twice and is scared that if he begins charters, his guests may have problems as well. During Hurricane Ana, in 2014, the yacht became "suspiciously waterlogged," even though he took all necessary precautions to make sure the boat survived the storm. It has become too much for him after all of these years, and he has put the *Splendor* up for sale.

So far there has not been much interest in the yacht, but Nelson is hopeful that a museum will buy it and preserve it. He said that he has done some small repairs and has spent ten years doing renovations. He went on to say that the stateroom where Wood and R. J. slept still contains many of the same tiles and the same blue bed remains in the exact spot where it was the night Natalie died. The initials, WW are still engraved into the captain's chair.

Two Harbors has changed little since Natalie Wood's death: the pier where Wagner, Walken, and Wood came ashore remains the same; the mooring where Captain Davern tied up the *Splendor* is still there as if awaiting the boat's return; even Doug's Harbor Reef Restaurant is still the only place to dine at the Isthmus (however, the name Doug's has been removed). Two Harbors is one of those quintessential yachting towns where tradition is respected and where the love of those traditions remains; it is also a place where Natalie Wood remains.

The cove where Natalie Wood's body was found is just a short walk down the beach from the town itself. There have been numerous reports over the years since her death of people seeing a woman walking along the beach of Blue Cavern Point, always in the direction of Two Harbors. This wraith is dressed the same in every report: She is seen wearing a nightgown and argyle socks but no shoes. The one exception is that sometimes she is wearing a bright red jacket, and other times she is not. It is assumed that this is the apparition of Natalie Wood since the specter is wearing the same clothes that the actress was wearing when her body was found. It is believed that the spirit of

Wood is trying to reach the town but always seems to have a bewildered look on her face as if she is lost and a bit confused. Witnesses claim that they get a feeling of sadness and loss when they gaze at the ghost, and as they watch, the woman simply fades from view and is gone.

The town itself has had many tales told over the years about Natalie Wood's spirit returning. Most of the stories take place in the cold, winter months of November and December, but what these witnesses tell are pretty much the same tales as those who have seen her at Blue Cavern Point. They claim that they have seen Natalie walking down the main road of Two Harbors heading directly for the center of town; again, the ghost is described as wearing a long nightgown and a red jacket; however, in most of these tales she is wearing what appears to be a pair of boot-style fur slippers. The witnesses have all said that they watch her move towards the Harbor Reef Restaurant until she walks through the closed door of the café. Could Natalie be trying to find her husband, R. J., in the building or perhaps just looking for help? We may never know.

The Harbor Reef has also had its share of Natalie Wood sightings. This differs from the other visions in that she has been seen sitting at an empty table but appears to be having a good time with unseen companions. She is usually wearing what is described as "casual boat attire." Many believe that this is a simple residual haunting brought on by her final night of happiness before her death later that evening.

We may never truly know what actually happened on that fateful November night in the lovely Catalina cove known as The Isthmus. It is hard to believe that someone so deathly afraid of the water and who couldn't swim would have taken a dinghy out to get away from an argument, and no one really wants to believe that Robert Wagner could have killed his wife or that Walken, one of the most respected actors of his time, could have murdered his co-star out of jealousy. But one thing is certain, on that night we lost a beautiful, shining star, and her name was Natalie Wood.

CHAPTER 11

JOHN BELUSHI

John Belushi's Walk of Fame star at 6355 Hollywood Boulevard.

Fame and fortune do not always translate into happiness and contentment; in fact, they can often become the opposite of this and drive someone into the depths of despair or into the waiting arms of drugs and alcohol. This is exactly what happened to one of the brightest stars of the 1970s and early 1980s, when, in a depressed state and with the aid of a vulture who hoped to increase her own stature, he died from a massive overdose. Even today, his spirit haunts the room where he died just as his memory and talents live on in the annals of Hollywood legend. I am speaking, of course, about John Belushi.

John Belushi was born on January 24, 1949, in Chicago but grew up on the outskirts of the Windy City in the town of Wheaton. John's father was a restaurateur who owned two establishments and always thought John would take over the family business when he grew up; John had far different plans for his future, however. John was always a wild sort, and this led him to the high school football team where he excelled; he became co-captain of the team, was elected homecoming king his senior year, and was all set to receive a scholarship when he decided the stage was where his heart was leading him. Belushi had performed in the variety shows at school and even in a couple of plays where, with a bit of encouragement from his drama teacher, he put aside his aspirations to become a football coach and decided instead to pursue an acting career.

After high school, Belushi performed in summer stock in rural Indiana, and his ability to play any part given him from serious to comedic gained him instant recognition from his peers. Unfortunately, Belushi began to change in his freshman year at the University of Wisconsin; he grew his hair long and began to foster a bad-boy image by skipping classes and having discipline problems. He dropped out of the University shortly afterward and moved back to Wheaton where he attended the College of DuPage, a junior college just a few miles from home. John's father, thinking his son had no future, began trying to convince his son to take an interest in his restaurants. John would not hear of it and formed the West Compass Players so he could hone his talents for comedy and acting. This improv group was patterned after the Second City comedy ensemble already famous in Chicago. The following year, 1971, Belushi was asked to join the cast of Second City; it is here his career took off.

In his time as a Second City cast member, John Belushi met Harold Ramis, Chevy Chase, and Christopher Guest, and then, in 1974, he met cast member Dan Aykroyd. During this time, Belushi and long time girlfriend, Judith Jacklin, were married. Judith became one of the producers of the show, and it seemed as if their lives couldn't get any better. Then, he tried out for a new show to be aired on NBC; the producers of the new show, *Saturday Night Live*, were leery of the flamboyant and somewhat over-the-top style of Belushi and kept him waiting for a long time before they finally brought him in for his audition. When they saw the raw talent and charismatic charm of Belushi, he was hired on the spot.

The characters that Belushi created for the show were some of the most beloved to ever arise in the more than forty-year history of the show. His Samurai Futaba, Pete Dionasoplis of the Olympia Café, a killer bee, and of course his unforgettable portrayal of "Joliet" Jake Blues from the movie *The Blues Brothers* are characters that people even today mimic and copy, and those either too young to remember or not even born at the time know of him. Belushi's performances on *Saturday Night Live* brought him to the attention of a young director by the name of John Landis, who was casting a new movie about college life seen through the eyes of the most party-happy fraternity on campus. Landis needed someone to play the small part of an obnoxious but lovable college student, and Belushi was the perfect fit for the character in *Animal House*. His performance of Bluto in the film was spectacular, and even though it was a character with few scenes and even fewer lines, Belushi stole the show, and Bluto became the most memorable character to come out of the movie.

Riding the wave of success from *Animal House*, Belushi appeared in a string of unsuccessful films but with some big name pull: *Goin' South* with Jack Nicholson and Mary Steenburgen; *Old Boyfriends* with Talia Shire; and *1941* with *Saturday Night Live* co-star Dan Aykroyd and directed by Steven Spielberg. Every one of these films was billed as a hit, but each was a flop with audiences. Belushi hit a personal low and sunk into a fit of depression. His drinking got worse, and he started using drugs to help him cope with what he began to believe was his failure to achieve his dream of stardom. The one bright spot in Belushi's career was the band that he and Aykroyd had formed in 1978 called *The Blues Brothers*. The duo had not only created a musical sensation but alter egos to go with it. Dan Aykroyd's Elwood complimented Belushi's "Joliet" Jake Blues perfectly, and the way the two played off each other with a seriousness born of comedy made the characters instantly likeable.

Their first album, *Briefcase Full of Blues,* reached number one on the *Billboard* charts and reached double platinum with two singles, "Rubber Biscuit" and "Soul Man", reaching thirty-seven and fourteen (respectively) on the *Billboard* top one hundred. Both Aykroyd and Belushi left *Saturday Night Live* in 1979 to pursue movie and musical avenues. They combined to bring their alter egos to the screen with the 1980 release of the feature film *The Blues Brothers*. The John Landis-directed film became a cult favorite and, while not an instant success, was one of the best received movies of 1980. While Belushi and Aykroyd were the stars of the film, it also featured some of the greatest blues and soul artists of the time, names such as Aretha Franklin, John Lee Hooker, Ray Charles, Henry Gibson, and the inimitable James Brown, who were all a draw for audiences both young and old.

As much as Belushi loved going on stage with his friend and performing as The Blues Brothers, John's dream was to make it big as an actor. His next two films were again disappointments. In *Continental Divide*, Roger Ebert said of his performance: "He had a surprising tenderness and charm," but most of the reviews for the film were tepid, and the box office numbers were decidedly mediocre. His next project reunited him with Aykroyd in the film *Neighbors*. The decision for Belushi to play the straight man to Aykroyd's zany, Bluto-like character was doomed from the start. The audience could not comprehend the switch in demeanor, and it was reflected in the abysmal box office take. These two failures to capture both the audience and the recognition as a star actor seem to have sent John Belushi into a downward spiral that he would never recover from.

John Belushi had been a casual drug user for most of his life; there were also times when his alcohol consumption would get out of control, especially at bars where fans and hangers-on would buy him copious amounts and watch him entertain the whole room until he was asked to leave. Through all of this, however, his drug use had remained relatively within the casual realm. The last six years of his life saw a dramatic change in this pattern, and near the end of his life it grew to addict status. The reasons for this increase were most likely due to Belushi's perceived failure at attaining the status he desired, even though in the eyes of his fans and many others he had achieved his goal and more—but in his own eyes he had fallen short. John was not blind to his failings, and after the death of his grandmother, had tried for more than a year to get clean—with some success—but then the pressures of Hollywood and the stage caused him to relapse. This became a cycle of sobriety and substance, sobriety and substance, until his eventual death. Belushi would hire "trainers" to help him cope with the addiction, but like most addicts, those he sought help from just became another crutch to lean on and were never truly able to give him what he needed. It was one of these trainers, Bill "Superfoot" Wallace, who found Belushi the day he died.

John Belushi's next film project was a screwball comedy titled *Noble Rot*, with a script adaptation written by Belushi and his *SNL* co-star Don Novello, who was well known for his portrayal of Father Guido Sarducci. The film was to be the vehicle Belushi needed to achieve stardom in the wake of the disastrous films he had just been featured in. To get the project off the ground and running, Belushi had to split time between his home in New York and Los Angeles, where the film was to be made. His wife, Judy, was worried that her husband was wearing himself thin and had noticed that he seemed to be relying on drugs more and more to help him cope with the strain of launching the film, and being away from her for long periods meant she couldn't help take care of him.

On his last trip to Hollywood, John Belushi rented a bungalow at the exclusive Chateau Marmont on Sunset Boulevard, an upscale and reclusive hotel for the Hollywood elite. Belushi had been using a lot of cocaine to help keep him going during the hectic work schedule, and quite a few people were helping him obtain the drugs—most for their own ends as a way of using Belushi's star status for their personal gain.

Cathy Smith first met John Belushi in 1976 on the set of *Saturday Night Live* when The Band was the scheduled musical guest. Smith had a long career being involved with several music groups and singers. She had even had a longtime affair with singer/song writer Gordon Lightfoot; the affair led Lightfoot to write the song "Sundown," which became his only number one hit and was about his fears of Smith and his feelings for her. At the time of Belushi's death, Smith had sunk so low as to become a full-time drug dealer, and it was Smith who Belushi relied on to supply him with his cocaine while he was in Hollywood.

The night of March 4, 1982, John Belushi was partying with friend and fellow comedian Robin Williams and in need of drugs. Belushi called Cathy Smith to come over with a new supply, and when she showed up, John asked her if she wanted to hang out with them for a while. Robin Williams had always disliked Smith and had said about her, "She was a lowlife that just creeped me out." Williams decided to leave for the night rather than stay with Smith and Belushi. Cathy Smith had not only shown up with cocaine in her possession, she had also brought along heroin and had convinced John to try a "speedball." This was a combination drug of cocaine and heroin that was injected with a syringe. John had always been leery of needles so Smith injected him. At some time during the night, close friend Robert De Niro stopped by, but noticed that Belushi was intoxicated and "not quite himself" and left without closely checking on his friend's actual condition. Belushi and Smith continued to party for a while longer until Smith decided it was time to head home.

The next morning Bill Wallace tried to phone Belushi but could get no answer. They were supposed to have met earlier for a workout, and Wallace was beginning to worry. When he arrived at the Chateau Marmont to check on his friend, there was no response to his knocks at the door. He tried the knob, found it unlocked, and entered the bungalow. There he found Belushi lying on the bed in a fetal position, sheets twisted around him, his body grossly discolored from where the blood had pooled inside his corpse, and with his tongue hanging out of his mouth. Bill Wallace knew immediately that his friend was dead. Cathy Smith was called to the scene but after being questioned was released. The official coroner's report stated the cause of death as "acute cocaine and heroin intoxication." John Belushi was dead at the age of thirty-three and by all accounts from an accidental overdose . . . which may not be the case.

After the furor died down, Cathy Smith moved to St. Louis where her lawyer, Robert Sheahen, told her to avoid reporters at all costs. After the press found her, she fled back to Los Angeles, then went to New York where she lived until finally moving back to her hometown of Toronto, Canada. By the time she was back home, new evidence had come out about her involvement in Belushi's death, and she was extradited back to the United States and charged with first-degree murder. Smith finally admitted that it was she who had injected Belushi with the speedball, not once, not twice, but eleven times; the prosecutor argued that with the amount of alcohol and drugs found in Belushi's system that he had most likely not been able to comprehend the amount of drugs Smith was injecting him with and, therefore, not responsible for what happened. Smith alone had caused his death.

As happens with so many of these cases, before the trial could begin Cathy Smith was offered a plea deal; Smith accepted, pled guilty to involuntary manslaughter and several drug charges, and spent fifteen months in the California Institute for Women, a prison in the central valley. Smith was released in March of 1988 and was promptly deported back to Canada where she worked as a legal secretary; she was subsequently arrested in 1991 for heroin possession.

PARANORMAL ASSOCIATION

John Belushi, by all accounts led a very successful life. He will always be remembered as the funny man from *Saturday Night Live* and *Animal House*; he will be known as the talented partner of Dan Aykroyd in the music duo The Blues Brothers, and will forever be known as one of the rising stars of the 1970s and 1980s. What is sad, however, is that John Belushi will also be known as a drug addict who overdosed on speedballs.

The Chateau Marmont. This upscale, exclusive hotel where John Belushi died is tight lipped about all of their guests, both living and dead.

As much as we think we know about Belushi's life, there is even more that eludes us: What drove him to abuse drugs and alcohol? Why did he look at his life and think, "I need to do more?" and in death must be thinking, "Why do people believe I would inject so many drugs when I was on the verge of stardom?" This last question, combined with his probable murderer still running free may be why Mr. Belushi has not crossed over and is still with us in spirit today.

The Chateau Marmont was built in Hollywood as a place where movie stars and the elite could go and not have to worry about losing their privacy, and that tradition holds even today. The management and staff at the luxury hotel are tight lipped and refuse to talk about any of their current or past guests, but that hasn't stopped the reports of John Belushi's ghost appearing at bungalow 3 from getting out to the public. It would seem that John has stayed in the room where he died and is still entertaining guests. One of the most widely told stories involves a couple who were staying in bungalow 3 with their young son. The boy was a bit restless that night and stayed awake talking to someone who the parents believed was imaginary. The boy kept talking and laughing all night until he finally fell asleep near dawn. A couple of years later, while watching TV the boy called to his mother and pointed to the screen telling her, "That's the funny man from the hotel." The child was pointing at a picture of John Belushi. When the mother called the Chateau Marmont and found out that the room they had stayed in that night was the same one Belushi had died in, she was stunned.

Another couple who stayed the night in the room said that they kept getting an eerie feeling of being watched; it got so bad that neither could walk down the hallway near the bathroom and rear bedroom alone. When they would shower, the other would have to stay in the bathroom and neither could look in the mirror for fear of what would be looking back at them. They never did see anything, but the feeling was so strong they just knew that they were never alone in the room. When they found out that it was Belushi's room, they just laughed as they loaded their luggage into the car.

The mirror is a common complaint of people staying in bungalow 3. The front desk has had so many calls from guests staying in that room who have complained about the "feeling" they are being watched from the mirror that they have had to move many guests to different rooms. The same feeling of being watched and of never quite being alone in the room has been reported often ever since Belushi's tragic death. Other reports from the hotel include windows opening and closing, furniture moving, strange noises, and voices when no one is present. There have even been reports of a floating head and the feeling of someone getting into bed with guests, even though no one can be seen.

The Chateau Marmont reportedly isn't the only place where John Belushi's spirit has been felt. Longtime friend and creative partner Dan Aykroyd has said many times that he can feel John's presence in Studio 8H. This is the studio where *SNL* was taped and one of the places where Belushi had some of his best moments while alive. Aykroyd has said that: "It's as if John is in limbo here." John's spirit has also been seen in Martha's Vineyard where he was buried. His grave had been moved once by his wife as a way to prevent destructive fans from harming the site, and even though his grave remained in the same cemetery John may be confused by the duality of the stones.

John Belushi was a great talent and his improv genius could have taken him far. He made us all laugh and smile, which is something we could all use more of. When you think about Belushi, try not to think about how he died but of how he lived and strove for something elusive in his art that we couldn't see. For whatever drove him forward may have been for his own peace of mind but it would have led to our enjoyment and would have lifted our spirits in a world that can sometimes drive us all just a little crazy.

TUPAC SHAKUR AND BIGGIE SMALLS

University Medical Center in Las Vegas. Tupac was brought here after he was shot and where he died a few days later.

People have called rap many things over the years—dangerous, violent, poetic, misogynistic, and harmonizing—but one thing it has been called and has proven itself to be, is deadly. In the early days of the genre, the music was almost tame in its poetic cadence of spoken word set to a rhythmic beat, but as the 1990s dawned, a new trend was coming awake in the rap community. Artists found that they could use rap music as a way to express their grievances and dissatisfactions with the unfairness of life they felt was all around them. Their music was aggressive, fierce, some would say brutal, but in the minds of the young people performing and those listening, it was also honest and true. Into this maelstrom Tupac Shakur and Chris Wallace, AKA Biggie Smalls, Notorious B.I.G, would wade, two of the most talented and respected artists of their time and two of rap's Original Gangstas.

Tupac was born Tupac Amaru Shakur on June 16, 1971, to a former Black Panther activist who had spent time in jail while pregnant with her son. She chose the name because it meant "shining serpent" in Incan, and his mother, Afeni, once said while in prison that, "My son is going to save the black nation."

Tupac grew up in the Bronx, New York, and even though they were poor, Afeni made sure that her son was bright, well-mannered and most of all, educated. If young Tupac got out of line, his punishment would be to read the *New York Times* front to back, and while her son never really enjoyed it, it made him aware of what life in the world was like starting at a young age. Two years after Tupac was born, Afeni gave birth to his sister, Sekyiwa. Her father, Mutulu Shakur, the man whose name Tupac had assumed, was a Black Panther and had been in and out of jail while Tupac grew up. He would eventually be sentenced to sixty years in prison while Tupac was still young. His godfather, convicted murderer Geronimo Pratt, was serving a life sentence in California. The future rap star would grow up without a stable father figure. The closest the young man had was Afeni's lover, a man nicknamed "Legs," who was a small-time drug runner and dealer for a Harlem drug lord.

As time went by, money became an issue, and life in New York became hard. Afeni moved her two children to Baltimore where a data processing job awaited her. Afeni was determined to give Tupac the best education available, and through hard work and a lot of door knocking, managed to get him into the prestigious Baltimore School for the Arts. Before moving from New York, Afeni had enrolled Tupac in a Harlem theatre troupe where he stared in *A Raisin in the Sun* at the Apollo Theatre; by the time he was thirteen he knew that acting was something he would pursue later in life. "I didn't like my life," Tupac said. "But through acting I could become somebody else." It didn't take long for Afeni to realize that Tupac and his sister were growing up rough on streets that could kill her babies, and in an attempt to protect them, sent them to Marin County, California, to spend the summer with her friend. It wasn't long after they arrived that Afeni got a call and was told she needed to come pick her kids up because her friend was entering rehab the next day.

When Afeni arrived, the "safe haven" she thought she had been sending her kids to turned out to be just as bad, if not worse, than the neighborhood she had tried to get them away from. Afeni had been hiding the fact that she had become a crack-addict from her children, but it didn't take long for Tupac to figure it out. And at the age of seventeen, he moved out on his own. He still attended high school, the affluent Mt. Tamalpais High; however, they were unaware that he was now on his own. Tupac moved into an abandoned apartment with a few other boys and supported himself with delivering pizzas. The money was bad, his life was not going the way he wanted it to, and it wouldn't be long before he embarked into another line of work.

Christopher Wallace was born in Brooklyn, New York, on May 21, 1972, and grew up in the Bedford-Stuyvesant neighborhood surrounded by drug dealers and addicts. It didn't take long before the young Wallace was introduced to gangs and joined one in his early teens. He gave himself the nickname Biggie Smalls because he was the biggest one in his gang; he was an imposing figure around the neighborhood, but even so, Biggie said that, "Hustlers were my heroes."

By the time Biggie was seventeen, he became a drug courier and during a drop had been arrested for dealing crack; he was sentenced to nine months in a North Carolina jail. After his release, Biggie went back to New York. Not wanting to continue with the life that, in his eyes, had chosen him, Wallace started making music and got together with a group named Old Gold Brothers. He borrowed a friend's four-track tape recorder and began recording hip-hop demos in the basement where he lived. Once Biggie had a good sampling of his music, he began to distribute the tapes to local New York radio stations where his music was played and came to the notice of a young, up-and-coming music producer by the name of Sean "Puffy" Combs.

Biggie Smalls became Notorious B.I.G under Sean Combs and, with two covers of Mary J. Blige's *"Real Love"* and *"What's the 411"*, along with his single, "Party and Bullshit," featured on the soundtrack for the film *Who's the Man*, Notorious B.I.G. was now on the road to stardom. With "Puffy" Combs at the helm, Biggie released his debut album, *Ready to Die*, under the Bad Boy label, and the record quickly skyrocketed to platinum on the charts. That same year, *The Source* named the young rapper, "Best New Artist" and "Best Live Performer" as well as "Lyricist of the Year." As Biggie's fame grew, the one thing that didn't change was his desire to help his friends and his ability to not forget where he came from. Wallace always remembered the hard streets and those who helped him out of his troubled times. It was at this time in his life that he met another star hip-hop artist and one who he would forever be linked to, for better or for ill.

Once Tupac Shakur was on his own, he realized that delivering pizza and working odd jobs was not going to get him anywhere. He began selling crack cocaine, and even though the money was coming in from this venture, it wasn't what he had dreamed for his life. His friends would tell you that no matter where Tupac was—at a local 7-11 store, hamburger joint, or club—he would be busy writing down songs on a napkin, or the back of a receipt, or anything else he could use to jot down his lyrics. He would chase girls, write poetry, and study his textbooks, but what Tupac really wanted was to be a performer.

He and his roommates formed a group they called the One Nation Emcees, and Shakur started skipping class—he was just about to graduate when he left school for good. Tupac soon moved to Los Angeles at the invitation of one of his mother's friends, and he briefly worked with a man organizing youth groups, but soon found that there were too many politics involved, and, with songs running through his head, went back to pursuing a music career. Tupac got a try out with a group called Digital Underground

(D.U.), impressed them, and was signed on the spot. He started out as a roadie, then graduated to dancer, and finally was given his chance at the mic; once there his commanding presence and talent got him the notice of everyone who saw him. Tupac began recording solo tunes and, when he finally had enough for an album, began the work of getting them released. One of the problems in Tupac's mind was the sterilized, happy rap that D.U. was performing. Gangsta was coming on the scene and that was what everyone wanted to hear. Tupac knew he needed to change his image.

Before Tupac Shakur had the chance to restyle himself, on a whim, he tried out for a part in a film called *Juice*. The director and producer were so impressed with his dry read that they cast him in the part on the spot. The film was shot in Harlem, and Tupac's performance, according to producer Neil Moritz, was, "Dynamic, bold, powerful, and magnetic—any word you want to use." Moritz went on to tell Tupac that within ten years he was going to be a big star. Tupac Shakur's response was ominous and prophetic when he said, "In ten years, I'm not going to be alive."

Once back in Los Angeles, Tupac's manager was just about to close a deal with Interscope Records when they heard two songs by the artist: one about a father's love and the other about the joys of shooting it out with cops. They immediately signed him to their label. Tupac began writing songs at a fever pace, so many in fact, that the album *2Pacalypse Now* was released well before anyone would have expected. It sold 5,000,000 units and when *Juice* was released in the theaters shortly after the record, Tupac almost became a household name. One person who noticed Shakur was a hulking, six-foot-three, 355-pound mountain of a man by the name of Marion "Suge" Knight.

Tupac Shakur and Biggie Smalls had met while Tupac was in New York on business and became friends. Smalls would call Shakur and ask for advice and Tupac was happy to give him what knowledge he could; he felt that all of the artists at that time should stick together and promote each other as a way of advancing the growing rap movement. At the same time, "Suge" Knight was busy trying to get Tupac to move to his label, Death Row Records, but so far had been unable to get him to sign a contract. Tupac, trying to live up to — or down depending on your viewpoint — his Gangsta reputation had been in and out of trouble with the law for quite some time, and it came to a head when Tupac was charged with sodomy, rape, and weapons possession when a nineteen-year old who he had sex with came back the next day and was assaulted by members of Tupac's entourage in his hotel room while Shakur was in the other room. While awaiting the trial in New York, Tupac received a text to come down to Quad Studios in Times Square to record a rap track; the studio was paying him $7,000, and in need of money due to the trial, Shakur readily agreed, even though he had no idea who had sent him the message.

When Tupac and his companions arrived at the studio, they pressed the intercom and were relieved to hear a voice they recognized come over the speaker; it was an associate of Notorious B.I.G., so they figured it must have been Tupac's friend or his manager, "Puffy" Combs, who had sent him the text message. Tupac's group entered the building and headed for the elevator; they were about to press the button when two young black men appeared, both brandishing pistols and one called out, "Don't nobody move. Everyone on the floor." Tupac froze in place as his friends dropped to the ground. When the two gunmen saw Tupac still standing, one of them said: "Shoot that Motherfucker!" Five shots rang out, and Tupac was hit in the head, hand, and his testicle. The gunmen then grabbed as much of Tupac's gold and jewelry as they could and ran out the door. As Tupac was being loaded into the ambulance, Biggie Smalls and Sean Combs exited the elevator; when Tupac saw them he flipped them off while mouthing the words, "Fuck you!" Tupac was convinced that the two East Coast rappers had set him up to be robbed and killed to get rid of him as competition.

Luckily, Tupac had not been seriously injured by any of the bullets, and he was released the following afternoon from the hospital. The rape trial continued, and Tupac was cleared of the more serious charges of sodomy, rape, and weapons possession; he was convicted, however, on three lesser charges of "sexual touching without consent." Because of his past convictions and run-ins with the law, the judge sentenced Tupac to four-and-a-half years in a maximum-security prison. His lawyers filed an appeal and tried to raise the $1.3 million bail the judge had set but were having trouble raising that kind of cash. That's when Suge Knight stepped in with an offer that Tupac couldn't refuse.

While Tupac was sitting in prison he came to the realization that his life was spinning out of control. He told his friend that, "I didn't rape that woman, but I didn't stop it, either. I need to show people my true heart. I'm going to show them the man my mother raised me to be." It was this thought that Tupac kept in his mind when Suge Knight came to him and offered him a contract, telling him that he would pay his bail, and Tupac could pay him back by recording his songs. Tupac jumped at the chance to get out of prison to begin showing the world who he really was. Tupac had demanded a house for his mother, which Suge agreed to, and then had his attorney whip up a contract that gave control of Tupac's business affairs over to Suge and made Suge's lawyer Tupac's legal representative; Tupac scanned the contract and then put his name to it.

Even though Tupac had vowed to change his life, he still hadn't forgiven Biggie Smalls for the perceived attempt on his life. A year to the day after Tupac had been shot in New York, one of the friends who had been with Shakur that day was found murdered execution style on a Queens, New York, street, followed by a fight between Suge's and Puffy's crews, with guns drawn, at the Soul Train Awards. Suge Knight, Biggie, and Combs all denied any animosity between them and also denied any involvement in the shootings, but Tupac wouldn't let it go. In a song released by Death Row, the rapper taunted Biggie by including the lyrics, "I fucked your bitch, you fat motherfucker." This was the catalyst in what became known as the East Coast-West Coast Rap War.

Tupac's music was selling well, movie scripts kept coming in, and his schedule became hectic. Even with all of this, Tupac still found time to write his songs, poetry, scripts, and even started a couple of books. He found time to tutor and to look after two children who had been orphaned in a drug killing. He also took a murdered friend's daughter to her high school prom; he even found time to dance with a wheelchair-bound female fan one night at the House of Blues. Tupac said that his biggest change came from his fiancé, Kidada Jones, daughter of famed musician, composer, and producer, Quincy Jones.

Christopher Wallace had noticed that when the so-called "war" started between him and Tupac that record sales skyrocketed. Biggie never responded to any of Tupac's threats or insults but admitted that during that time he feared for his own life. Violence had sprouted up between the fans on both sides of the country and Biggie didn't want to get caught in the crossfire. To try and end the feud between them, Wallace made a trip out to Los Angeles in 1995, to attend the MTV Awards with the intent of talking to Tupac at the after party. When Shakur saw Wallace at the party, he stormed up to Biggie, leaned in close and told him, "I'm just trying to sell some records." Tupac, ever the showman, had used the "war" as a way to promote a bad boy image to boost sales.

Even though Tupac was selling a lot of records, most, if not all of the money had been going to Knight and Death Row Records. The contract that Shakur had signed had all but guaranteed that he would not see much money. His records had made just over $60 million but Knight said that Tupac still owed him close to $5 million for "services" that had been provided. The bail money, the house that Tupac was living in, travel provided by the company for business trips was all charged to Tupac's account. There is even speculation that Knight was paying the New York crime syndicate out of Tupac's earnings. All Shakur knew was that he wanted out, he was tired of playing Suge Knight's games, was tired of playing the gangster role; he wanted more for himself and the family he intended to start with Kidada, and he told Knight as much.

In early September of 1996, Tupac traveled to New York to attend an awards show. Kidada assumed that he would be his typical self and bed a woman or two while away from home but was pleasantly surprised when she received a call from him the first night and said, "I can't do that anymore; I'm all yours." Then he hung up the phone saying, "I'd take a bullet for you." He was back in Los Angeles a few days later but seemed distracted and not himself. Kidada asked him what was wrong and he told her that he had promised Suge that he would accompany him to the Tyson fight being held at the MGM Grand in Las Vegas, but that he really didn't want to go and had a bad feeling about the trip. He asked her to come along, and even though she couldn't attend the fight, he felt that if she were with him in Vegas everything would be all right. Kidada kissed him and told him she would love to be with him on the trip.

The night of the fight, Tupac arrived at Suge Knight's Las Vegas mansion where Tupac and Suge, along with Suge's entourage partied before heading out to the MGM Grand. The fight only lasted 109 seconds. Suge said that they would head over to his private club and finish out the evening there. As the group was leaving the venue, a man, later identified as a Crips gang member, approached and began harassing Suge

The corner at Koval and Flamingo where Tupac was shot waiting at a red light. The pole in the foreground is where Tupac's ghost is often seen leaning.

and Tupac. Suge Knight had close ties to the Crips' main rival gang, the Bloods, and apparently the young man had decided to put forth his colors. A fight broke out with the Crip being beaten badly by Tupac with the help of some in Knight's group. After a brief stop at the Luxor so Tupac could get cleaned up, they headed over to Club 662. Tupac rolled the passenger window down in Suge's BMW, and at one of the stop lights, a paparazzi snapped a picture of the rapper; this would be the last photo of Tupac to be taken while the young man was still alive. Just two red lights later, a white Cadillac with California plates pulled up alongside the BMW; a gun was pointed out the window and a hail of bullets sped towards Tupac's body. The rapper frantically tried to escape into the back seat but was hit in the chest by two bullets; another hit him in the pelvis and one in his hand.

The Cadillac sped away when the pistol's magazine was finally empty. As Tupac was carried into the emergency room at the hospital, he looked at those who were wheeling him in and said, "I'm dying." Six days later, on September 13, 1996, his prediction would come to pass.

Who killed Tupac Shakur is still unknown. Was it the Crips seeking revenge, East Coast rappers, Suge Knight's enemies or his friends, or Suge himself to keep Tupac from leaving Death Row Records and signing with someone else? Quite a few even believed it was Biggie Smalls in an act of vengeance for everything Tupac had put him through during the Rap Wars. This line of thinking may be one of the reasons that Biggie's life was on borrowed time from the moment Tupac was killed.

After Tupac was murdered, Biggie admitted that he was scared for his life but was determined to try and put an end to the East Coast–West Coast rivalry. In an attempt to do just that, Biggie attended a few events in Los Angeles to let his fans and the fans of the West Coast rap crowd know that he had forgiven them and hoped that they would do the same for him. On March 7, 1997, Biggie attended the Soul Train Music Awards. It was a way for him to not only let fans know that he was with them but to promote his next album, *Life After Death*. While in Los Angeles, Wallace had received a call stating that if he attended the *Vibe* magazine after party at the Peterson Automotive Museum the following day that "he was a dead man." Sean Combs talked Biggie into going anyway, and that evening the party became so raucous and crowded that the Fire Marshal had to break it up. Biggie and a group of friends went to get the car while his wife, Faith Evans, waited at the front of the museum to be picked up. While standing there, she heard what sounded like gunshots and then screams when the bystanders realized what was happening.

When Wallace and his entourage were driving to the front of the museum, they had to stop for a red light. As they waited for the light to change, a green car pulled up next to Biggie's SUV; a few people jumped out and several shots were fired before the group got back into the car and it sped away. Biggie was hit several times while none of the other passengers in the car were harmed. Wallace died almost instantly and was pronounced DOA when he arrived at Cedars-Sinai Medical Center; he had been transported there in his own, bullet-riddled car. In just over six months' time, rap music had lost two of its brightest and most promising performers to assassins' bullets. Tupac Shakur was only twenty-five years old when he died , and Christopher Wallace, AKA Biggie Smalls, AKA Notorious B.I.G., was only twenty-four when he was gunned down. Gangsta Rap had certainly earned its bad boy reputation.

Neither Tupac's nor Biggie's murders have ever been solved. There has been much speculation regarding both shootings, and as mentioned above, most people believe, at least on the West Coast, that Biggie was involved or at least had knowledge of Tupac Shakur's killing. As far as Biggie's murder, the prevailing theory is that Marion "Suge" Knight had the East Coast rapper killed. A shooting between two Los Angeles police officers occurred shortly after Wallace's murder—one officer appeared to have been living with Knight's girlfriend at Knight's mansion, and the other cop, who was involved in the investigation of the rapper, links Knight to the killing. As there is circumstantial evidence that the LAPD may have been involved in a cover-up having to do with other officers who were working as security for Knight—all against department rules—along with the evidence suggesting the slugs found in the rapper's body were police issue and that those same officers were involved in the "Rampart" scandal later on, one can decide for themselves what they want to believe. All of the mystery, the cover-ups, and the speculation, along with no one ever being held accountable for the violent deaths of the two rap artists, may be one of the reasons they have not found rest and are still seen by people even today.

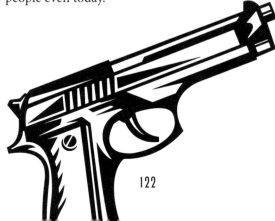

Biggie Smalls' spirit has been seen on occasion outside of the museum where he was shot to death. His violent murder may have caused an imprint in the area surrounding the Peterson Automotive Museum. This "residual" type of haunting is common with murder victims, but because Biggie was gunned down while riding in his SUV, one wonders why his spirit is seen walking along the sidewalk out front. Speculation has it that since he had to leave his wife, Faith Hill, so he could retrieve the car, his ghost is looking for her in the afterlife.

It was at the exit from this garage where shots rang out
mortally wounding Biggie Smalls.

Another place that Biggie is often seen is at the recording studio in New York where he recorded most of his music. This studio has had so many reports over the years that it has become an urban legend in its own right. The studio has even called in ghost hunters to try and find out what it is that Smalls wants and to hopefully allow him to move on. On more than one occasion, a musician or singer will be in the process of recording when a voice will call out into their headphones distracting them enough to ruin the track or recording they are working on.

One of Biggie's former girlfriends and a star in her own right, Lil' Kim, has said that the rapper had been coming to her in her dreams for a while, but that when the movie about his life, titled *Notorious,* was released that Biggie Smalls actually appeared to her to complain about the film. Lil' Kim said in an interview to *Rap Radar* that Smalls was "not satisfied" with the film but, "has love for everyone involved with the film." After its release in 2009, the film had widespread appeal, and at least one psychic came out and said that the movie itself had awoken Biggie's spirit and that it was causing him to haunt the places he would frequent. The clairvoyant went so far as to state that Biggie Smalls could appear to his more fervent fans, drawn by their love and devotion to him and his music. This author is leery of this claim but will leave it to readers as to what they believe.

Tupac Shakur was gunned down while sitting in Marion "Suge" Knight's BWM waiting at a red light at the corners of East Flamingo Road and Koval Lane. It took him six days to pass away from his wounds, and almost immediately after the young man died reports began coming in of people seeing Tupac hanging around the corner where he was shot. Those who have witnessed the rapper have said that he looks as if he is lost and will often stand on the corner closest to where the BMW was waiting at the light when the bullets rang out. Others have said that, as they have stood there staring, the sound of gunfire would ring out, and then the sound would fade away, and the rapper would vanish from sight. Still other people have said they have seen Tupac simply leaning against the light pole. They would go on to say that he would look over at them, give them one of his bright smiles, and then disappear.

Another place where Tupac is often seen is at the mansion that Suge Knight owned in a trendy area just outside of Las Vegas. Many people have seen the rapper standing on the second-floor balcony, leaning against the rail and staring out at the darkened neighborhood. The claims are always the same from one witness to the next: they will see the young man standing there in seeming contemplation, and then, as they watch, the figure will simply fade from view. The residents who live in the neighborhood all know about the ghost, and many of them have actually seen the proof for themselves. Tupac would rarely stay at the mansion when he was in town; he preferred hotels and was never a big fan of his manager, who he believed was using him. But at least, in death, it would seem Tupac likes the solitude the area provides over the crowded Las Vegas Strip where he would stay in life.

Tupac liked to stay at the Luxor Hotel when he was in Las Vegas for concerts or business. This is the hotel where he and his fiancée, Kidada Jones, were staying the night he was killed. The Luxor is known for its luxury, architecture, and, lately, its paranormal rooms. One of these rooms is the one where Tupac was staying on that fated night in September 1996 when he was brutally gunned down. Some believe that the rapper still hangs out in the room, perhaps looking for the love of his life, Kidada, in the hopes of reuniting with her.

The hit Travel Channel show *Ghost Adventures* features three paranormal investigators, Zak Bagans, Nick Groff, and Aaron Goodwin, who travel to locations and televise their investigations into the unknown. The three stars live in Las Vegas and filmed an episode of the show at Madame Tussauds at the Venetian Hotel. During their investigation, they stated that they encountered some physical manifestations and unusual readings on their equipment near the wax figure of Tupac Shakur and may have recorded some EVPs (electronic voice phenomenon) of the slain rapper. Tupac was attacked only a couple of blocks away from where his wax figure is displayed, so it could be that his spirit is there trying to make himself known.

In an interview with *TMZ*, rapper DJ Quick said Tupac haunted him one day during a recording session at Legendary Studios. Quick told *TMZ* that while he and Pac affiliate Big Syke, were in the "Karen Carpenter Room," so named because the legendary singer is known to haunt the room, that Tupac made himself known. He goes on to say that Syke leaned back in his chair during a break in recording, lit a blunt, and for no discernible reason began to laugh. DJ Quick said that the laugh coming from Syke was not his but that of Syke's old friend, Tupac Shakur. He said the lights got a little weird, and he suddenly got the chills. Quick believes that Tupac was there and was having some fun with them.

Another rapper who may have seen Tupac's spirit is Kendrick Lamar. He said that one evening after a long recording session, as he was trying to sleep on his mother's couch, Shakur appeared to him with a message. He said Tupac told him: "Don't let the music die." He said he heard him say the words "clear as day," and that it was, "like he's right there. Just a silhouette."

The hole that the deaths of both Tupac Shakur and Biggie Smalls left in the rap music world still have not been filled, even to this day. The schism between East Coast and West Coast rap has grown smaller but still persists, albeit minor. The fans of both young men are loyal to a fault, and both men are still spoken of in the same way as Elvis Presley is by an older generation. The legends surrounding Tupac are the same that have sprouted up about the king of rock and roll with Tupac sightings springing up all over the world, and talk of the rapper finally coming out of hiding to let his fans know that he is still alive. As for Christopher Wallace, urban legend has a new Bloody Mary story: it is said that if you stare into a mirror and call out "Biggie Smalls" three times that he will appear but without the deadly intent of his counterpart.

Neither man is who they were and are portrayed to be. Biggie Smalls was a man who had been thrown into a life of crime, just as Tupac had, by a set of circumstances beyond their control. Biggie pulled himself out with his music, never really wanting to be a Gangsta or live that lifestyle. Tupac, with a mother who made sure to bring her son up right and give him a good education, was highly intelligent and brilliant when it came to writing and acting, but fell victim to a culture that tried to drag him down into the abyss before he found his way through his mother's faith and love. Unfortunately, both men died before their true potentials could be realized, and even though this author is a hard-core rock 'n'roller, I can't help but wonder what we have missed by their passing from this reality.

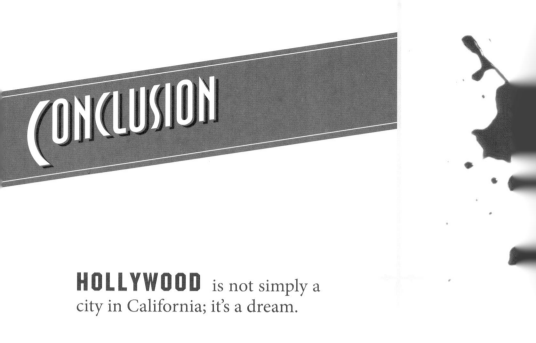

CONCLUSION

HOLLYWOOD is not simply a city in California; it's a dream.

And at the same time it can become a nightmare. People from all walks of life flock to the cameras, some to be stars, others, like Bugsy, to make trouble and elicit handfuls of cash. One thing they all have in common is that they are human, and as such, they are never free from the reaper, or from the vail that he commands.

BIBLIOGRAPHY

GEORGE REEVES

http://cecilbuffington.com
www.hollywood.com
www.jimnolt.com
www.paranormal-encounters.com
www.phantomsandmonsters.com
www.prairieghosts.com
www.varietyportal.com

THELMA TODD

http://myloveofoldhollywood.blogspot.com
https://thesilentmovieblog.wordpress.com
http://u1.netgate.net/~jlatham/Todd_Table.html
www.prairieghosts.com/hollywood8.html

LOS FELIZ MURDER MANSION

http://articles.latimes.com
http://fultonhistory.com
http://m.sfgate.com
http://mylabucketlist.com
https://ironysupplement.wordpress.com
https://news.google.com
www.sciencedirect.com

THE BLACK DALIHA

http://downtownla.com
http://lmharnisch.com/home.html
www.geni.com
www.biography.com
www.edhat.com
www.prairieghosts.com
www.todayifoundout.com

MARILYN MONROE

https://marilyn4ever.wordpress.com
https://m.youtube.com
www.marilynmonroepages.com
www.vanityfair.com
http://radio.foxnews.com
http://hauntedtahoe.blogspot.com
http://patch.com
www.hauntedhouses.com

BENJAMIN SIEGEL

http://classiclasvegas.squarespace.com
https://joebrunoonthemob.wordpress.com
www.biography.com
www.history.com

RAMON NOVARRO

http://articles.latimes.com
http://ghosthuntnow.com
http://m.imdb.com
www.altfg.com
www.out.com
www.silentsaregolden.com
www.tcm.com

MANSON MURDERS

http://allday.com
http://cielodrive.com
http://law2.umkc.edu
http://www.mirror.co.uk
https://books.google.com
https://en.m.wikipedia.org/?title=Charles_
    Manson
www.biography.com
www.franksreelreviews.com/shorttakes/
    sharontate.htm
www.ghostplace.co
www.laweekly.com
www.lostinthegrooves.com
www.rottenworks.com

NATALIE WOOD

http://arlindo-correia.com
www.cnn.com
http://documents.latimes.com
http://losangeles.cbslocal.com
http://articles.latimes.com
www.dailymail.co.uk

JOHN BELUSHI

http://m.imdb.com
http://moviepilot.com
http://traveltips.usatoday.com
www.biography.com
www.franksreelreviews.com
www.slate.com

TUPAC SHAKUR AND BIGGIE SMALLS

Oberding, Janice. *Haunting of Las Vegas*. Pelican
    Publishing, 2008.
Papa, Paul W. *Haunted Las Vegas*. Globe Pequot
    Press, 2012.
http://m.imdb.com
http://truthabouttupac.com
www.biography.com
www.kazzledazz.com
www.theguardian.com
www.vanityfair.com